9/10/14
$24.95
B&T

BETTER *from* SCRATCH

· ·

IVY MANNING

PHOTOGRAPHY BY ALICE GAO

weldon**owen**

CONTENTS

ABOUT THIS BOOK

From crisp, quick refrigerator pickles to peak-of-season fruit preserves, from healthful, flavorsome snacks to showstopping party bites, from popular condiments to classic cocktail fixings, this inspired recipe collection offers easy formulas for putting together scores of favorite foods from scratch.

Making the foods you typically buy means you can skip the artificial flavors, preservatives, and generous additions of sodium, sugar, and fat that store-bought foods use to ensure shelf life and profitability. In contrast, these recipes rely on healthful, nutritious ingredients, such as seasonal produce, high-quality olive oil, and local meats and seafood, to make everything you eat tastier and better for you. Preparing foods at home also allows you to customize flavors for everyday fare like granola, energy bars, salsas, and salty snacks.

Not only are homemade crackers, confections, cured meats, jams, and soft cheeses more healthful but they are also easier on your budget. When you cook from scratch, you are not paying extra for elaborate packaging, marketing, and distribution, which translates to more money in your pocket at day's end.

None of the recipes in this book calls for fancy tools or equipment. A traditionally outfitted kitchen holds everything you'll need. You'll find recipes for every skill set and time constraint, too, from three-ingredient treats like crunchy, curry-spiced Kale Chips to more time-consuming Limoncello and Sauerkraut, which require extra attention—and include a fun lesson in kitchen science. All of the recipes are easier to make than you might initially think, however. Expend a little effort and you'll be rewarded with food that tastes so much better than its store-bought kin that you'll be asking yourself, "Why haven't I made this before?"

In these pages, you'll find recipes that fit every occasion and time of day. For breakfast ideas, turn to nutritious Strawberry Almond Granola or apple-and-nut Energy Bars, or tuck into pancakes that you make from your own Gingerbread–Spiced Apple Pancake Mix and then smear with heavenly Pear-Cardamom Butter at the table. Or, elevate your morning toast with a spoonful of Pear-Ginger Jam or Classic Orange Marmalade.

When lunchtime rolls around, dress up your sandwiches with homemade versions of such pantry staples as ketchup made from garden-ripe tomatoes, aioli flavored

PREPARING FOODS AT HOME ALSO ALLOWS YOU TO CUSTOMIZE FLAVORS FOR EVERYDAY FARE LIKE GRANOLA, ENERGY BARS, SALSAS, AND SALTY SNACKS.

with Meyer lemon juice, or salt-cured bacon smoked over wood chips—your BLTs will never be the same again. Or, turn to the recipes for Sauerkraut and Beer Mustard for a memorable Reuben, and to creamy homemade Horseradish and Pickled Salmon Bites for Norwegian-style open-faced sandwiches on rye.

You'll discover a host of recipes perfect for dinnertime, too, including such international-inspired condiments as Thai-style Sriracha hot sauce for zesty stir-fries, sweet-tart Italian Mostarda di Frutta for roast meats, and naturally fermented Kimchi for Korean noodles and fusion tacos. Plus, you can update classic supper fare with an assortment of better-than-bought everyday ingredients, like creamy homemade ricotta for lasagna, a trio of salsas for taco night, and nutritious Kale Pesto for a quick weeknight pasta meal.

Exceptional nibbles for entertaining are here, as well. Guests will marvel at your kitchen savvy when you serve homemade Membrillo with slices of Manchego, silky Aquavit and Dill-Cured Lox on rye, or Classic Olive Tapenade with crostini. They'll never guess that you simmered the Membrillo in the slow cooker, that the lox takes just minutes of prep and a few days of unattended curing, or that the tapenade is as easy as turning on a food processor. At-home mixologists are sure to appreciate the handful of unique bar recipes, like lemongrass-infused tonic syrup, three-citrus Margarita Mix, a quartet of Simple Syrups, and nicely tart cocktail onions.

Nearly everyone enjoys receiving a handmade gift, and many of these recipes are perfect for giving. From homespun s'more kits composed of spiced Graham Crackers and Vanilla Marshmallows to Buttermilk Corn Bread Mix paired with a jar of savory Bacon-Onion Jam, your friends will love getting presents from you because they were made in your kitchen.

With the recipes in this book as a guide and the wealth of beautiful color photographs for inspiration, you'll soon discover how much better everything tastes when it's made from scratch. When that happens, you'll be well on your way to becoming a true food artisan.

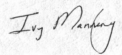

PICKLES
& PRESERVES

QUICK DILL PICKLES

SOME THINGS, LIKE THESE CRISP DILL PICKLES, ARE CLASSIC FOR A REASON. IF YOU ARE NEW TO PICKLING VEGETABLES, START WITH THIS STRAIGHTFORWARD RECIPE. MAKE THE PICKLES AT THE HEIGHT OF SUMMER, WHEN SMALL KIRBY CUCUMBERS AND HEADS OF FRESH DILL CAN BE FOUND AT FARMERS' MARKETS.

Distilled white vinegar, 3 cups (24 fl oz/750 ml)

Kosher salt, 2 tablespoons

Kirby cucumbers, 12–14

Pickling spice, 6 tablespoons (1½ oz/45 g)

Dill, 18 mature heads, or 6 tablespoons (1½ oz/45 g) dill seeds plus 24 fronds fresh dill leaf

Garlic, 24 cloves

Peppercorns, 36

MAKES 6 ONE-PINT (16-FL OZ/500-ML) JARS

Have ready 6 sterilized jars and their lids.

Mix the vinegar, 3 cups (24 fl oz/750 ml) water, and salt in a pot and bring to a boil. You may need more brine, so have extra vinegar on hand.

Cut the cucumbers into slices ½ inch (12 mm) thick. In the bottom of each jar, place 1 tablespoon pickling spice, 3 dill heads or 1 tablespoon dill seed (use 4 fronds dill leaf against the glass for visual effect), 4 cloves garlic, and 6 peppercorns. Layer the cucumber slices in the jars, making sure to stack them closely, with no large voids. Fill the jars to within 1 inch (2.5 cm) of the rim with cucumbers.

Once the brine boils, ladle the brine into the jars, leaving ½ inch (12 mm) of headspace. Slide a metal chopstick or other thin tool down the side of each jar, between the glass and the cucumbers, four or five times. This will release any air bubbles. Adjust the headspace, if necessary, then wipe the rim of each jar clean. Tighten the lids firmly but do not overtighten.

Refrigerate the pickles for at least a few hours before serving, to allow the flavors to develop. They will keep for up to 3 weeks.

DILLY BEANS

THESE BEANS ARE PHENOMENAL IN BLOODY MARYS; ADD A DASH OF THE BRINE TO YOUR DRINK FOR AN EXTRA PUNCH. "SPICY" MEANS DIFFERENT THINGS TO EACH INDIVIDUAL, SO IF YOU'RE A HEAT LOVER, DOUBLE THE AMOUNT OF CAYENNE IN EACH JAR. IF NOT, YOU CAN OMIT THE CAYENNE ALTOGETHER.

Distilled white vinegar, 3 cups (24 fl oz/750 ml)

Kosher salt, 6 tablespoons (2 oz/60 g)

Dill, 6 heads, or 6 tablespoons (2¾ oz/80 g) dill seeds plus 24 fronds fresh dill leaf

Cayenne pepper, 1½ teaspoons

Garlic, 6 cloves

Fresh green beans, 4 lb (2 kg)

MAKES 6 ONE-PINT (16-FL OZ/500-ML) JARS

Have ready 6 sterilized jars and their lids. Mix the vinegar, 3 cups (24 fl oz/750 ml) water, and salt in a pot and bring to a boil.

In each jar, put 1 dill head, or 1 tablespoon dill seeds and 4 fronds of fresh dill, ¼ teaspoon cayenne, and 1 clove garlic. Wash the beans and trim to the height of your jars, leaving ½ inch (12 mm) headroom. Pack the beans as tightly as you can into the jars. It may help to start packing the beans while holding the jar horizontally or to use a small spatula to press the beans to the side as you put in more beans.

Pour the boiling brine into the jars, leaving ½ inch (12 mm) of headspace. Slide a metal chopstick or other thin tool down the side of each jar, between the glass and the beans, four or five times. This will release any air bubbles. Adjust the headspace, if necessary, then wipe the rim of each jar clean. Tighten the lids firmly but do not overtighten.

Refrigerate the beans for at least a few hours before serving, to allow the flavors to develop. They will keep for up to 3 weeks.

SAUERKRAUT

FOR A COLORFUL VARIATION, ADD 1 CUP (3½ OZ/105 G) PEELED, SHREDDED CARROTS TO THE SAUERKRAUT BEFORE PACKING IT INTO THE JARS. FOR A CARAWAY FLAVOR, MIX 3 TABLESPOONS CARAWAY SEEDS WITH THE CABBAGE BEFORE FERMENTATION. ENJOY WITH SAUSAGES AND ON SANDWICHES OR SALADS.

Place the cabbage in a large bowl, sprinkle with the salt, and toss to combine. Cover and let stand until softened, about 30 minutes.

Working in batches, tightly pack the cabbage into a 4-qt (4-l) ceramic crock or food-grade plastic tub. Add any accumulated liquid from the bowl. Cover the cabbage with cheesecloth, set a plate on the cloth, and top with heavy weights. Cover the crock with a kitchen towel and let stand at room temperature. Within 24 hours, the cabbage should be submerged in brine. If it isn't, stir 1 teaspoon salt into 1 cup (8 fl oz/ 250 ml) water and add to the crock. Check the cabbage every day or two. If scum forms, scrape it off and rinse the plate before returning it. Depending on the temperature, the cabbage will ferment in 10 days to 4 weeks. It is ready when bubbles no longer appear and the aroma is pleasantly pungent, usually about 2 weeks. Taste, and if it is too mild, let it continue to ferment.

Sauerkraut fermentation is an evolutionary process. The flavor will become more concentrated as the weeks go by. Using tongs or a large spoon, remove a serving or a jarful at a time and re-cover the crock. If you remove more than you can use at one time, refrigerate the remainder in a separate container. Conditions can vary from batch to batch, depending on how cool the storage environment is, but after several weeks the sauerkraut will lose texture and be less tasty. Try to work through your crock in 4 weeks.

Red and/or green cabbage, 5 lb (2.5 kg), tough outer leaves removed, quartered, cored, and finely shredded

Kosher salt, 3 tablespoons, plus extra if needed

MAKES 8 ONE-PINT (16-FL OZ/500-ML) JARS

PICKLED VEGETABLES

YOU CAN PICKLE PRETTY MUCH ANY VEGETABLE, SO CUSTOMIZE YOUR SELECTION BASED ON WHAT'S IN SEASON AND PERSONAL PREFERENCE. DON'T OVERLOOK LESS FREQUENTLY PICKLED ITEMS ITEMS LIKE WATERMELON RADISHES AND FENNEL. SERVE ON A CHEESE PLATE, WITH COCKTAILS, OR AS A GARNISH FOR PANINI.

Trim the radishes, carrots, haricots verts, wax beans, and okra. Cut the celery into 4-inch (10-cm) lengths and cut the radishes in half. Place the vegetables in a large heatproof bowl.

In a small saucepan, combine the vinegar, sugar, salt, mustard seeds, star anise, and peppercorns over high heat and bring to a boil, stirring to dissolve the sugar. Pour the hot vinegar mixture over the vegetables, making sure they are submerged. Let cool, tossing the vegetables frequently. Cover and refrigerate for at least 2–4 hours before serving. The vegetables will keep for up to 3 weeks.

Mix of vegetables, such as French Breakfast radishes, baby carrots, haricots verts, wax beans, and/or okra, about ¼ lb (125 g) each

Celery, 4 stalks

White wine vinegar, 2 cups (16 fl oz/500 ml)

Sugar, ½ cup (4 oz/125 g)

Sea salt, 2 teaspoons

Yellow mustard seeds, 2 teaspoons

Star anise pod, 1, broken into pieces

Peppercorns, 6

MAKES ABOUT 1¼ POUNDS (625 G)

PICKLED SALMON BITES

THIS EASY METHOD OF PICKLING FISH IS PERFECT FOR ENTERTAINING—JUST
A FEW DAYS OF UNATTENDED BRINING PRODUCES A JAR OF ROSY SALMON BITES
INFUSED WITH SWEET-TART FLAVOR. SERVE AS PART OF A SMORGASBORD
WITH BUTTERED RYE BREAD AND HOMEMADE HORSERADISH (PAGE 120).

**Wild salmon fillet, 1 lb (500 g),
preferably from the thicker,
collar end of the fish**

Kosher salt, 1 tablespoon

**Distilled white vinegar, 1 cup
(8 fl oz/250 ml)**

Sugar, ¼ cup (2 oz/60 g)

**Yellow mustard seeds,
1 tablespoon**

Pickling spices, 2 teaspoons

**Star anise pod, 1, broken
into pieces**

**Shallots, ¾ cup (3 oz/90 g),
thinly sliced**

Lemon, ½, thinly sliced

**MAKES 2 ONE-PINT
(16-FL OZ/500-ML) JARS**

Have ready 2 sterilized jars and their lids.

Remove the skin from the salmon, cut the flesh into ¾-inch (2-cm)
cubes, and toss with the salt in a nonreactive bowl. Cover and
refrigerate overnight.

In a nonreactive saucepan, combine 1 cup (8 fl oz/250 ml) water,
the vinegar, sugar, mustard seeds, pickling spices, and star anise
over high heat and bring to a boil. Reduce the heat to medium-low
and simmer the brine for 5 minutes. Pour the mixture into a large
measuring cup with a spout, set aside, and let cool completely.

Rinse the salmon chunks with cold water and pat dry. Layer the
salmon, shallots, and lemon slices in the jars. Pour the cooled brine
mixture over the salmon. Screw the lids on the jars, shake gently
to distribute the spices, and refrigerate for 2 days before serving.
The salmon will keep in the refrigerator for up to 2 weeks.

KIMCHI

KIMCHI, THE NAME USED FOR A BROAD ARRAY OF PICKLED KOREAN VEGETABLES, IS A DELICIOUS ADDITION TO SOUPS, SALADS, AND STIR-FRIES. HERE'S A RECIPE FOR SMALL-BATCH KIMCHI THAT'S HOT BUT NOT TOO SPICY, WITH NICE CHUNKS OF CRUNCHY DAIKON AND A HINT OF SWEETNESS FROM ASIAN PEARS.

Have ready 2 sterilized jars and their lids.

Cut 1 inch (2.5 cm) off the root end of the cabbage and discard. Quarter the cabbage lengthwise. Cut the quarters crosswise into strips 1 inch (2.5 cm) wide, plunge them into a large bowl of cold water, and drain. In a large bowl, toss the cabbage and daikon with the salt. Weigh the vegetables down with a few heavy plates and let stand for about 5 hours. Rinse the cabbage and daikon briefly with cold water and drain well.

In a large bowl, combine the cabbage, daikon, pear, green onions, Aleppo pepper, chile powder, sugar, fish sauce, garlic, and ginger. Toss well to coat the vegetables with the seasonings. Transfer the mixture to the jars.

Push the vegetable mixture down in the jars. Cover the jars with plastic and leave them at room temperature for 1–4 days. Taste the kimchi once a day and push the vegetables down as needed so the brine rises to cover. When the kimchi is fermented to your liking, screw on the lids and refrigerate. The kimchi is best used within 3 weeks. After 3 weeks, you may notice the kimchi has a pronounced sour, fizzy flavor. It is still edible at this stage and traditionally used in soup where the sourness is diluted with broth.

Napa cabbage, 1 small head (about 1 lb/500 g)

Daikon radish, ½ lb (250 g), peeled, quartered lengthwise and sliced ¼ inch (6 mm) thick

Sea salt, 1 tablespoon

Asian pear, 1, peeled, cored, and chopped

Green onions, ½ cup (1½ oz/45 g) chopped, including tender green tops

Aleppo pepper or red chile flakes, 1 tablespoon

Mild New Mexican chile powder, 1–2 tablespoons

Sugar, 2 teaspoons

Fish sauce, 1 tablespoon

Garlic, 1 tablespoon chopped

Fresh ginger, 1 tablespoon peeled and finely chopped

MAKES 2 ONE-PINT (16-FL OZ/500-ML) JARS

PICKLED COCKTAIL ONIONS

THESE TINY WHITE GLOBES LOOK SO BEAUTIFUL IN THE JAR, YOU MAY NOT WANT TO OPEN IT. BUT ONCE YOU DO AND BITE INTO YOUR FIRST ONION, YOU'LL WANT TO USE THE ONIONS NOT ONLY IN CLASSIC COCKTAILS BUT ALSO IN SALADS, ON ANTIPASTO PLATTERS, AND AS ACCOMPANIMENTS TO SLICES OF SHARP CHEESE.

Pearl onions, 1½ lb (750 g)

Malt vinegar (5% acidity), 2 cups (16 fl oz/500 ml)

Kosher salt, 1 tablespoon plus 1 teaspoon

Bay leaves, 6

Yellow mustard seeds, 2 tablespoons

Peppercorns, 2 tablespoons

MAKES 6 HALF-PINT (8-FL OZ/250-ML) JARS

Have ready 6 sterilized jars and their lids.

Fill a large bowl with ice water. Bring a large saucepan of water to a boil and add the onions. Boil for 2 minutes, drain, and plunge them into the ice water. Using your fingers and a paring knife, peel away the skins and discard.

In a large nonreactive saucepan, combine the vinegar, salt, and 2 cups (16 fl oz/500 ml) water and bring to a boil over medium-high heat, stirring to dissolve the salt.

Meanwhile, in each jar, place 1 bay leaf, 1 teaspoon mustard seeds, and 1 teaspoon peppercorns.

Pack the jars with the peeled onions to within ¾ inch (2 cm) of the rims. Ladle the hot brine into the jars, leaving ½ inch (12 mm) of headspace. Slide a metal chopstick or other thin tool down the side of each jar, between the glass and the onions, four or five times. This will release any air bubbles. Adjust the headspace, if necessary, then wipe the rim of each jar clean and seal tightly with a lid.

Refrigerate the onions for at least a few hours before serving, to allow the flavors to develop. They will keep for up to 3 weeks.

TIPSY COCKTAIL GARNISHES

WHY USE TOP-SHELF LIQUOR, SPECIALTY BITTERS, AND VINTAGE GLASSES AND THEN GARNISH YOUR CREATIONS WITH RUN-OF-THE-MILL GARNISHES? IF YOU PRIDE YOURSELF ON MAKING TRULY EXCELLENT COCKTAILS, YOU MUST TRY THESE SIMPLE PICKLES. THEY'LL PUT THE BLING IN YOUR BARTENDING.

Pearl onions, 1 cup (4 oz/125 g)

Garlic, 3 large heads

Green cherry tomatoes, 1¼ cups (8 oz/250 g)

Lemon zest, 3 strips, each 2 inches (5 cm) long

White wine vinegar, 1½ cups (12 fl oz/375 ml)

White vermouth, 1½ cups (12 fl oz/375 ml)

Sugar, 3 tablespoons plus 2 teaspoons

Dried chamomile flowers, 1 tablespoon

Coriander seeds, 1 tablespoon

Sea salt, 1½ teaspoons

Fennel seeds, 1½ teaspoons

Bay leaves, 3

MAKES 3 ONE-PINT (16-FL OZ/500-ML) JARS

Have ready 3 sterilized jars and their lids.

Cut the top ¼ inch (6 mm) off the tip of each onion and trim the root ends just to remove the exterior roots, leaving the hard root core intact so the onions won't fall apart during cooking. Break apart the garlic heads, separate the cloves, and discard the papery outer skins but do not peel the cloves themselves. Stem the tomatoes.

Fill a large bowl with ice water. Bring a large saucepan of water to a boil and add the onions and garlic. Boil for 2 minutes, drain, and plunge them into the ice water. Using your fingers and a paring knife, peel away the skins and discard.

Divide the onions, garlic, tomatoes, and lemon zest strips evenly among the jars, leaving 1 inch (2.5 cm) of headspace at the top.

Combine the vinegar, vermouth, sugar, chamomile flowers, coriander seeds, salt, fennel seeds, and bay leaves in a large nonreactive saucepan and bring to a boil over high heat, stirring to dissolve the sugar and salt. Turn off the heat and use a ladle to distribute the hot liquid and seasonings evenly among the 3 jars, leaving 1 inch (2.5 cm) of headspace.

Transfer the uncovered jars to the refrigerator. Once cool, screw the lids on the jars; they will keep refrigerated for up to 1 month. The onions and garlic will be ready to eat within 24 hours, and the tomatoes are best after 1 week. To serve, thread 1 tomato, 1 garlic clove, and 1 onion onto a toothpick or small skewer and place in your cocktail of choice.

TEQUILA JALAPEÑOS ESCABECHE

PICKLED JALAPEÑO AND CARROT SLICES MAKE AN IDEAL GARNISH FOR TEQUILA-BASED COCKTAILS, BLOODY MARYS, AND MICHELADAS, AND THEY'RE THE PERFECT PIQUANT ACCOMPANIMENT FOR MEXICAN FOOD. IF YOU'RE NOT A CHILE FAN, JUST REMOVE THE SEEDS FROM THE JALAPEÑOS.

Have ready 2 sterilized jars and their lids.

Wearing rubber gloves, slice off the stem from each jalapeño and discard. Cut the jalapeños crosswise into rings ¼ inch (6 mm) thick. For less heat, cut the jalapeños in half lengthwise, discard the core and seeds, and slice the halves crosswise into slices ¼ inch (6 mm) thick.

Divide the jalapeños, carrots, and garlic between the jars.

Combine ¾ cup (6 fl oz/180 ml) water, the vinegar, sugar, salt, coriander seeds, cumin seeds, oregano, and bay leaves in a saucepan and bring to a simmer over medium-high heat, stirring to dissolve the sugar and salt. Cook for 1 minute, remove from the heat, and add the tequila.

Ladle the hot vinegar mixture into the jars, leaving 1 inch (2.5 cm) of headspace. Transfer the uncovered jars to the refrigerator. Once cool, screw the lids on the jars; they will keep refrigerated for up to 2 months. Allow the vegetables to marinate for 1 day before serving.

Jalapeños, 10 ounces (315 g)

Carrot, 1 large, peeled and sliced into rounds ¼ inch (6 mm) thick

Garlic, 1 large clove, thinly sliced

Unseasoned rice vinegar, ¾ cup (6 fl oz/180 ml)

Sugar, 2 tablespoons

Sea salt, 2 teaspoons

Coriander seeds, 2 teaspoons

Cumin seeds, 1½ teaspoons

Dried Mexican oregano, 1 teaspoon

Bay leaves, 2

Silver tequila, ½ cup (4 fl oz/125 ml)

MAKES 2 ONE-PINT (16-FL OZ/500-ML) JARS

PRESERVED LEMONS

A STAPLE IN THE PANTRIES OF THE MIDDLE EAST AND NORTH AFRICA, PRESERVED LEMONS ARE A LEMON LOVER'S DREAM. ROAST THEM WITH CHICKEN, CHOP THEM UP AND ADD TO DIPS AND VINAIGRETTES, OR TOSS IN WARM PASTA DISHES. THIS SAME TECHNIQUE CAN BE USED TO MAKE PRESERVED LIMES.

Have ready 2 sterilized jars and their lids.

In a large nonreactive saucepan, bring 3 qt (3 l) water to a boil. Meanwhile, scrub each lemon thoroughly under cold running water to remove any dirt or wax. Add the lemons to the water, return to a boil, and cook until softened, 3–4 minutes. Remove with a slotted spoon and set aside to cool.

Cut each lemon lengthwise into quarters, leaving them attached at the stem end. Gently spread apart the quarters and sprinkle 1 tablespoon salt into the center. Place 1 tablespoon salt in each jar and pack the lemons into the jars. Pour in enough lemon juice to cover the lemons, leaving ½ inch (12 mm) of headspace. Seal the jars tightly.

Store the lemons in a cool, dark place for 3 weeks, turning the jars occasionally to distribute the lemon juice and salt evenly, before using. Then transfer the jars to the refrigerator to keep for up to 6 months.

Lemons, 10 firm, slightly underripe, preferably Meyer

Kosher salt, 12 tablespoons (4 oz/125 g)

Fresh lemon juice, 3 cups (24 fl oz/750 ml), or as needed

MAKES 2 ONE-QUART (1 L) JARS

CLASSIC ORANGE MARMALADE

REGULAR ORANGES ARE DELICIOUS HERE, BUT BLOOD ORANGES, WITH THEIR SWEET-TART JUICE AND SLIGHTLY BITTER PEEL, ARE ALSO FANTASTIC FOR MARMALADE. USE A MANDOLINE, IF POSSIBLE, TO SLICE THE ORANGES THINLY. DO NOT OVERCOOK THE MARMALADE OR IT WILL DEVELOP A CARAMEL FLAVOR.

Oranges, 2 lb (1 kg)

Sugar, about 6 cups (3 lb/1.5 kg), or as needed

Fresh orange juice, 2 cups (16 fl oz/500 ml)

Fresh lemon juice, ½ cup (4 fl oz/125 ml)

MAKES 7 HALF-PINT (8-FL OZ/250-ML) JARS

Have ready 7 sterilized jars and their lids. Place 2 or 3 small plates in the freezer.

Cut off the stem end of each orange. Slice each orange as thinly as possible, preferably on a mandoline. Place the slices in a large nonreactive saucepan and add 8 cups (64 fl oz/2 l) water. Bring to a boil over medium-high heat and cook uncovered, stirring frequently, for 15 minutes. Remove from the heat and let cool slightly.

Measure the orange slices and their liquid and return to the pan. For each 1 cup (8 fl oz/250 ml), add ¾ cup (6 oz/185 g) sugar. Stir in the orange and lemon juices. Bring to a boil over medium-high heat and boil rapidly for 10 minutes. Reduce the heat to medium and cook, stirring frequently, until slightly thickened and gelatinous, 7–10 minutes longer. Remove from the heat. Drop 1 teaspoon of the marmalade on a chilled plate; if it sets as it cools, the marmalade is ready. If not, return the pan to the heat and boil the marmalade for a few minutes longer, then test again.

Ladle the hot marmalade into the jars, leaving ¼ inch (6 mm) headspace. Slide a metal chopstick or other thin tool down the side of each jar, between the glass and the marmalade, four or five times. This will release any air bubbles. Adjust the headspace, if necessary, then wipe the rim of each jar clean and seal tightly with a lid.

Store the jars in the refrigerator for up to 1 month.

FIG PRESERVES

THE LUSH SWEETNESS OF FIGS SHINES THROUGH IN THIS SIMPLE RECIPE. ANY VARIETY WILL WORK: DARK-SKINNED FIGS PRODUCE AN ALMOST-PURPLE SYRUP; GREEN ADRIATIC FIGS YIELD A PALE SYRUP. FOR SOME SPICE, ADD A PINCH OF STAR ANISE. QUARTER THE FIGS AND SERVE ON CROSTINI WITH GOAT CHEESE.

Figs, 3 lb (1.5 kg), such as Black Mission, Adriatic, or Brown Turkey

Sugar, 4 cups (2 lb/1 kg)

Fresh orange juice, 1¼ cups (10 fl oz/310 ml)

Fresh lemon juice, ¾ cup (6 fl oz/180 ml)

Zest of 1 orange

MAKES 5 HALF-PINT (8-FL OZ/250-ML) JARS

Have ready 5 sterilized jars and their lids.

Trim the fig stems, leaving a little of the stem attached to each fig. In a large nonreactive saucepan, combine the sugar and orange and lemon juices over medium-high heat and bring to a boil, stirring to dissolve the sugar. Add the figs, reduce the heat to medium, and cook, stirring gently, for 5 minutes. Using a slotted spoon, transfer the figs to a bowl. Add the orange zest to the syrup and cook, uncovered, until reduced by one-third, 2–3 minutes. Return the figs to the pan and cook for 1 minute to heat through.

Using the slotted spoon, divide the hot figs evenly among the jars. Ladle the syrup over the figs, leaving ¼ inch (6 mm) of headspace. Slide a metal chopstick or other thin tool down the side of each jar, between the glass and the figs, four or five times. This will release any air bubbles. Adjust the headspace, if necessary, then wipe the rim of each jar clean and seal tightly with a lid.

Store the jars in the refrigerator for up to 1 month.

PEAR-GINGER JAM

THIS WINTRY JAM CAN BE USED AS AN ACCOMPANIMENT TO GINGERBREAD OR SPOONED OVER VANILLA ICE CREAM. THE BROWN SUGAR GIVES IT A DEEP CARAMEL FLAVOR, THOUGH YOU CAN USE ALL GRANULATED SUGAR IF YOU USE YOUNG, FIRM, FRESH GINGER FOR THE BRIGHTEST TASTE.

Have ready 5 sterilized jars and their lids.

In a large nonreactive saucepan, gently toss together the pears, fresh ginger, sugar, lemon juice, and the crystallized ginger, if using. Bring to a boil over medium-high heat, reduce the heat to medium, and cook uncovered, stirring frequently, until most of the liquid has evaporated and the jam is thick, about 10 minutes.

Ladle the hot jam into the jars, leaving ¼ inch (6 mm) of headspace. Slide a metal chopstick or other thin tool down the side of each jar, between the glass and the figs, four or five times. This will release any air bubbles. Adjust the headspace, if necessary. Wipe the rim of each jar clean and seal tightly with a lid.

Store the jars in the refrigerator for up to 1 month.

Pears, such as Comice or Warren, 3 lb (1.5 kg), peeled, cored, and cut into ½-inch (12-mm) cubes

Fresh ginger, 1 tablespoon, peeled and grated

Light brown sugar, 1 cup (6 oz/200 g), lightly packed

Fresh lemon juice, ¼ cup (2 fl oz/60 ml)

Crystallized ginger, 1 tablespoon finely chopped (optional)

MAKES 5 HALF-PINT (8-FL OZ/250-ML) JARS

STRAWBERRY JAM

SPREAD THIS JAM ON BREAD WITH AMARETTO ALMOND BUTTER (PAGE 69) FOR A DELICIOUS PB&J. TRY ADDING ¼ CUP (2 FL OZ/60 ML) BALSAMIC VINEGAR DURING THE LAST 3-4 MINUTES OF COOKING THE FRUIT. BE CAREFUL NOT TO OVERCOOK THE JAM, OR IT WILL TASTE CARAMELIZED.

In a large nonreactive bowl, gently toss together the strawberries, cherries, and sugar. Cover and let stand at room temperature for 1–2 hours.

Have ready 6 sterilized jars and their lids. Place 2 or 3 small plates in the freezer.

Transfer the fruit mixture to a large nonreactive saucepan and add the lemon juice. Bring to a boil over medium-high heat, reduce the heat to medium, and cook, uncovered, stirring frequently, for 10 minutes. Remove from the heat. Drop 1 teaspoon of the jam on a chilled plate; if it sets as it cools, the jam is ready. If not, return the pan to the heat and boil the jam for a few minutes longer, then test again.

Ladle the hot jam into the jars, leaving ¼ inch (6 mm) of headspace. Slide a metal chopstick or other thin tool down the side of each jar, between the glass and the jam, four or five times. This will release any air bubbles. Adjust the headspace, if necessary. Wipe the rim of each jar clean and seal tightly with a lid.

Store the jars in the refrigerator for up to 1 month.

Strawberries, 8 cups
(2 lb/1 kg), hulled and halved

Cherries, 2 lb (1 kg), pitted
and roughly chopped

Sugar, 2½ cups (1¼ lb/625 g)

Fresh lemon juice, ½ cup
(4 fl oz/125 ml)

**MAKES 6 HALF-PINT
(8-FL OZ/250-ML) JARS**

SNACKS
& SAVORY BITES

MASALA ROASTED CRISPY CHICKPEAS

THESE CRISPY NIBBLES GET THEIR EXOTIC FLAVOR FROM A HOMEMADE TOASTED SPICE BLEND CALLED PANCH PHORAN, OR "FIVE SPICES," THAT'S COMMONLY USED IN NORTHEASTERN INDIAN AND BENGALI COOKING. THE CHICKPEAS ARE BEST SERVED WARM AND CAN BE REHEATED IF MADE IN ADVANCE.

Place the cumin, fennel, nigella, mustard, and fenugreek seeds in a small, dry sauté pan over medium-low heat and heat the spices, stirring frequently, until they begin to give off a strong aroma, about 3 minutes. Pour the spices onto a small plate to cool, then transfer to a spice grinder or mortar and grind to a fine powder. Add the salt and cayenne and stir to combine. Set aside.

Pat the chickpeas thoroughly dry with paper towels. Line a plate with a double layer of paper towels. Heat the oil in a large sauté pan over medium-high heat until shimmering. Carefully add the chickpeas (they will spit and pop a bit) and fry, stirring frequently, until light brown and crisp, about 8 minutes.

Use a slotted spoon to transfer the chickpeas to the paper towel–lined plate. Sprinkle them with the spice mixture and serve immediately, or store in an airtight container at room temperature for up to 1 week. Reheat in a warm oven before serving.

Cumin seeds, ¼ teaspoon

Fennel seeds, ¼ teaspoon

Nigella seeds (black onion seeds), ¼ teaspoon

Yellow mustard seeds, ¼ teaspoon

Pinch of fenugreek seeds

Sea salt, ½ teaspoon

Cayenne pepper, ⅛ teaspoon

Canola oil, ½ cup (4 fl oz/125 ml)

Chickpeas (garbanzo beans), 1 (15-oz/470-g) can, drained and rinsed

MAKES 2 CUPS (8 OZ/250 G); SERVES 4–6

CHEESY CRACKERS

THESE IRRESISTIBLE BITES TAKE ONLY ABOUT 5 MINUTES HANDS-ON
TIME AND TASTE BETTER THAN ANY FANCY STORE-BOUGHT CRACKERS.
REFRIGERATING THE DOUGH ALLOWS THE FLAVORS TO MELD AND
MAKES THE LOG EASIER TO SLICE INTO NEAT ROUNDS FOR BAKING.

Comté or Gruyère cheese,
2 cups (8 oz/250 g) shredded

Parmesan cheese,
½ cup (2 oz/60 g) grated

Unsalted butter,
6 tablespoons (3 oz/90 g)

All-purpose flour,
1 cup (5 oz/155 g)

Pinch of cayenne pepper

Fresh chives, 2–3 tablespoons
chopped

Coarse sea salt, for sprinkling

MAKES 24-28 CRACKERS

In a food processor, combine the Comté and Parmesan cheeses, the butter, flour, and cayenne and process until well combined and crumbly, 40–60 seconds. Transfer the mixture to a sheet of plastic wrap and shape into a log about 2 inches (5 cm) in diameter and 6–7 inches (15–18 cm) long. Roll up the log in the plastic wrap, patting it to form a smooth, even cylinder. Refrigerate for at least 1 hour or for up to overnight.

Preheat the oven to 350°F (175°C). Unwrap the dough and slice into rounds about ¼ inch (6 mm) thick. Arrange on 2 ungreased, rimmed baking sheets, preferably nonstick, spacing them about 2 inches (5 cm) apart. Sprinkle the rounds evenly with the chives and top each with a pinch of salt.

Bake the crackers, 1 sheet at a time, until light golden brown, 10–15 minutes, rotating the pan front to back halfway through the baking time. For crispier crackers, bake for up to 3 minutes longer, watching carefully to avoid overbrowning. Serve right away.

KALE CHIPS

IT'S GREAT HOW SOMETHING AS HEALTHFUL AS KALE CAN BECOME AN
ADDICTIVE SNACK BY COATING THE LEAVES WITH OIL AND BAKING THEM.
I LIKE TO ADD CURRY POWDER AND MALT VINEGAR FOR EXTRA FLAVOR, BUT
THE CHIPS ARE GOOD PLAIN, TOO. COLLARD GREENS CAN BE SUBSTITUTED.

Kale, such as Lacinato or
Russian variety, 1 bunch,
about 1 pound (500 g)

Extra-virgin olive oil,
2 tablespoons

Curry powder, 2 teaspoons,
or 1 tablespoon malt vinegar
(optional)

Sea salt, ½ teaspoon

**MAKES ABOUT 6 CUPS
(16 OZ/500 G); SERVES 4**

Preheat the oven to 300°F (150°C). Line 2 baking sheets with
parchment paper or silicone baking mats. Tear each kale leaf
away from its central rib and stem, keeping the leaves in the largest
pieces possible. Wash the leaves in several changes of cold water,
spin dry in a salad spinner, and pat dry with paper towels.

Transfer the kale to a large bowl, drizzle with the olive oil, and
rub the oil into the leaves with your hands. Sprinkle the leaves
with the curry powder, if using, and toss to combine.

Arrange the leaves in a single layer on the prepared baking sheets.
They should be as flat as possible. (You may need to bake the kale
in batches.) Sprinkle the kale evenly with the salt.

Place the baking sheets on the top rack and lowest rack in the oven;
this will allow air to circulate between the pans and dehydrate the
leaves evenly. Bake until the kale is crisp and just beginning to brown
in places, 10–12 minutes, rotating the baking sheets once from top
to bottom and back to front.

The chips are best when served immediately. Store any leftover chips
in an airtight container at room temperature for up to 2 days and
reheat them in a 250°F (120°C) oven for 5 minutes to recrisp them.

THAI LIME LEAF SOY NUTS

THIS CRISPY SNACK WAS INSPIRED BY A TRIP TO THAILAND, WHERE I WAS DRAWN TO THE INCREDIBLE AROMAS OF A VENDOR FRYING PEANUTS, CHILES, AND KAFFIR LIME LEAVES. THIS RECIPE IS ENDLESSLY ADAPTABLE: SOY NUTS, CASHEWS, AND ALMONDS ALL TASTE GREAT WITH THIS ZESTY TREATMENT.

Place the soybeans in a large bowl and add cold water to cover by 3 inches (7.5 cm). Let soak overnight. Drain the beans, rinse well, and pat them dry with paper towels.

Preheat the oven to 300°F (150°C). Line a rimmed baking sheet with parchment paper or a silicone baking mat. Place the beans on the prepared baking sheet.

In a small sauté pan, heat the oil over medium-high heat. Add the lime leaves and chiles and sauté until the leaves and chiles turn golden brown, about 1 minute. Remove the pan from the heat. Using a fork, transfer the lime leaves and chiles to a small bowl. Set aside.

Pour the oil in the saute pan over the soybeans and stir to coat. Bake, stirring occasionally, until the beans are golden brown and crisp, about 1½ hours. Watch carefully the last 15 minutes to make sure they do not burn.

Transfer the soy nuts to a bowl. Crush the lime leaves and chiles with your fingers and sprinkle them over the nuts. Add a few generous pinches of salt and toss to combine. Let the nuts cool completely before serving. Store in an airtight container in the refrigerator for up to 2 weeks.

Dried soybeans, 2 cups (12 oz/375 g)

Canola oil, 2 tablespoons

Kaffir lime leaves, 10

Dried whole red chiles, 4, preferably árbol or Thai

Sea salt, for sprinkling

MAKES ABOUT 2½ CUPS (12 OZ/375 G); SERVES 4-6

SOUR CREAM & ONION POTATO CHIPS

THE PROCESS HERE IS SIMPLE: DEHYDRATE THIN POTATO SLICES IN A MICROWAVE AND THEN FINISH THEM IN THE OVEN, WHERE THEY BECOME DELIGHTFULLY CRISP. LOOK FOR BUTTERMILK POWDER IN THE BAKING AISLE OF MOST GROCERY STORES.

Preheat oven to 325°F (165°C). Line a large microwave-safe plate and 2 rimmed baking sheets with parchment paper. In a small bowl, combine the buttermilk powder, garlic powder, dill, salt, onion powder, and sugar and mix well. Set aside.

Using a mandoline, slice the potato crosswise into very thin slices (about ¹⁄₁₆ inch/2 mm thick). You should be able to see your fingers through a slice. Pat the potato slices dry with paper towels and arrange as many as will fit in a single layer on the prepared plate. Microwave on 90 percent power until the slices begin to curl around the edges and are dry to the touch, about 4 minutes. Transfer the slices, moist (bottom) side up, to a prepared baking sheet. Repeat with the remaining potato slices, replacing the parchment paper if it becomes moist.

Place the baking sheets on the top rack and the lowest rack in the oven and bake until the potato slices are golden brown and dry and crisp (no longer pliable) to the touch, 10 minutes, rotating the baking sheets once from the top to bottom and back to front. Some of the slices may need to cook for a few extra minutes. As the chips are done, immediately transfer them to a large bowl and mist them with the oil. When all of the chips have been misted, sprinkle them with the buttermilk mixture and toss to coat evenly.

Transfer the chips to a serving bowl and serve. Store any leftover chips in an airtight container at room temperature for up to 1 week.

Buttermilk powder, 1 teaspoon

Garlic powder, ½ teaspoon

Dried dill, ½ teaspoon

Sea salt, ½ teaspoon

Onion powder, ¼ teaspoon

Sugar, ½ teaspoon

Russet potato, 1

Olive oil, in a mister or food-grade spray bottle

**MAKES 6 CUPS (7 OZ/200 G);
SERVES 4-6**

RICOTTA CHEESE

THIS RECIPE YIELDS FLUFFY, RICH CLOUDS OF RICOTTA THAT TASTE SO GOOD
YOU WILL WANT TO EAT THEM WITH A SPOON LIKE ICE CREAM. FOR A MORE
REFINED SERVING IDEA, SCOOP THE RICOTTA ONTO A PLATE, TOP WITH
OLIVE OIL AND CRACKED RED PEPPERCORNS, AND SERVE WITH CRUSTY BREAD.

Whole milk, 4 qt (4 l)

Heavy cream, 2 cups
(16 fl oz/500 ml)

Distilled white vinegar,
¼ cup (2 fl oz/60 ml)
plus 2 tablespoons

Kosher salt, 1 teaspoon

MAKES ABOUT 4 CUPS
(2 LB/1 KG)

Pour the milk and cream into a large, heavy nonreactive pot, place
over medium-high heat, and heat to just below boiling. Stir with
a spatula to keep the liquid from scorching. Just before the milk
boils, the surface will start to foam and release steam. Check the
temperature and pull the pot off the heat just shy of 185°F (85°C).

Add the vinegar and stir for 30 seconds. The curds will form almost
immediately. Add the salt and stir for another 30 seconds. Cover
the pot with a dish towel and let the curds stand at room temperature
for 2 hours.

Line a colander with a large piece of cheesecloth, with the ends
overhanging the sides. Place the colander over a bowl to catch the
draining liquid. Using a slotted spoon, gently transfer the curds from
the pot to the colander. Let the ricotta drain for about 30 minutes.

Gather the cheesecloth by its corners and twist together to force out
the liquid. When the liquid turns from clear to milky and the cheese
starts to push through the cheesecloth, it has drained enough.

Remove the ricotta from the cheesecloth and store it in an airtight
container in the refrigerator. It's best when it is freshly made, but
it can be stored for up to 1 week.

MARINATED LABNE

THESE TANGY, CREAMY "CHEESE BALLS" ARE MADE BY SHAPING WELL-DRAINED YOGURT INTO SPHERES AND COATING THEM WITH ZA'ATAR, AN EARTHY HERB BLEND. SLATHER THIS TRADITIONAL MIDDLE EASTERN SPREAD ON WARM PITA OR BAGUETTE SLICES AND SERVE WITH A BOWL OF MARINATED OLIVES.

Dampen a thin dish towel with cold water, wring it out, and drape it in a bowl, with the ends overhanging the sides. In a separate bowl, combine the yogurt and salt and mix well. Spoon the yogurt into the center of the towel, then gather up the corners of the towel and tie them together securely with a long piece of kitchen string. Tie the string to a rack in the refrigerator and suspend the bag over a bowl to catch the drips. Alternatively, tie the bag to the handle of a sturdy wooden spoon, balance the spoon on the rim of a tall container or bowl, so the bag is suspended above the base of the container, and place the setup in the refrigerator. Let the bag hang for 48 hours, until the yogurt is the consistency of very thick cream cheese.

Line a small baking sheet with parchment paper. On a small plate, mix together the za'atar and paprika. Remove the bag from the refrigerator and open it. With lightly oiled hands, roll the yogurt into small balls about 1 inch (2.5 cm) in diameter. Work with a fast, light touch so the yogurt doesn't stick to your hands. If the yogurt is still too moist to shape, hang the bag in the refrigerator for another day. Roll the balls in the spice mixture and place them on the prepared baking sheet. Refrigerate the balls uncovered overnight to dry them further.

To serve, place the balls on a serving plate and drizzle them with a little olive oil. To store the balls, pour the 2 cups (16 fl oz/500 ml) oil into a widemouthed 1-pt (16–fl oz/500-ml) jar or other glass container, add the peppercorns, and then gently drop the balls into the jar. Cover and refrigerate for up to 2 months. Let come to room temperature before serving. The leftover spiced oil can be used for as a dip for bread or for cooking.

Plain full-fat yogurt,
2 lb (1 kg)

Sea salt, ¾ teaspoon

Za'atar, 2 tablespoons

Sweet paprika, 1 teaspoon

Extra-virgin olive oil, about 2 cups (16 fl oz/500 ml), if storing, plus more for drizzling

Black peppercorns, ½ teaspoon, if storing

MAKES 25 BALLS; SERVES 8 AS A SPREAD WITH BREAD

SEEDED CRACKERS

THESE CRISP CRACKERS CAN BE CUSTOMIZED BY USING DIFFERENT SPICES AND HERBS. ONCE THE DOUGH IS MADE, ROLL IT OUT, WRAP IT TIGHTLY IN PLASTIC WRAP, AND FREEZE THE SHEETS FOR UP TO 1 MONTH. WHEN YOU'RE READY FOR FRESH CRACKERS, JUST BAKE THE FROZEN SHEET FOR 20 MINUTES.

**All-purpose flour,
2 cups (10 oz/315 g), plus
extra for the work surface**

Sugar, 2 teaspoons

Salt, 2 teaspoons

**Coarsely ground pepper,
1 teaspoon**

Poppy seeds, 1 teaspoon

Sesame seeds, 1 teaspoon

Mustard seeds, 1 teaspoon

**Solid vegetable shortening,
1 tablespoon, at
room temperature**

**Unsalted butter,
1 tablespoon, cold**

**Heavy cream, ½ cup
(4 fl oz/125 ml), plus
extra if needed**

**MAKES ABOUT 30 SMALL
CRACKERS**

In a food processor, combine the flour, sugar, salt, pepper, and poppy, sesame, and mustard seeds and pulse 1–2 times to mix. Add the shortening and butter and pulse until the mixture forms large, coarse crumbs the size of peas, 7–10 times. Pour in the cream and pulse a few times until the dough comes together in a rough mass.

Scrape the dough onto a clean work surface and gently squeeze it together. Add a few more drops of cream if the dough will not hold a soft shape. Press the dough into a disk, wrap it in plastic wrap, and let rest at room temperature for at least 20 minutes or for up to 1 hour.

Preheat the oven to 350°F (180°C). Line 2 half-sheet pans with parchment paper.

Unwrap the dough and place on a lightly floured work surface. Cut the dough in half with a sharp knife. Roll out one-half of the dough into a rectangular sheet as thin as possible without tearing, dusting it with flour as needed to prevent sticking. Trim the edges of the dough to fit the prepared pan, then carefully transfer the dough to the pan. Repeat with the second half of the dough. Alternatively, using a pizza wheel or a sharp knife, cut the dough sheets into shapes and place on the pans.

Bake 1 sheet of crackers at a time until crisp and brown, 12–15 minutes. Transfer to wire racks and let cool completely until crisp. If you have baked the dough in sheets, break each sheet into shards. The crackers are best when eaten fresh, but they may be stored in an airtight container at room temperature for up to 5 days.

FOR VARIATIONS: See page 154.

BEEF JERKY

LONG BEFORE THE ADVENT OF REFRIGERATION, PEOPLE TYPICALLY DRIED AND CURED MEAT TO PRESERVE IT. BEEF JERKY IS AN EXAMPLE OF THIS TRADITION AND IS PROBABLY THE EASIEST PRESERVED MEAT FOR THE HOME COOK. THE RESULT IS FAR SUPERIOR IN TEXTURE AND FLAVOR TO THE STORE-BOUGHT PRODUCT.

Place the meat on a baking sheet and freeze it for 45 minutes, or until firm enough to slice easily. With a long, flexible, very sharp knife, cut the meat into slices ⅛–¼ inch (3–6 mm) thick, across the grain.

In a large, sturdy, resealable plastic bag, combine the soy sauce, bitters, liquid smoke (if using), hot pepper sauce, pepper, and garlic and onion powders. Add the meat slices in batches to the bag of marinade, massaging after each addition to coat both sides of each slice. Squeeze out most of the air from the bag and seal. Refrigerate for 6 hours but for no more than 8 hours. Turn the bag and massage it every 2 hours, moving the slices around. Drain the slices in a colander and discard the marinade. Blot both sides of each slice thoroughly dry with paper towels.

Line the floor of the oven with heavy-duty aluminum foil, covering it completely and folding up the edges of the foil to form a rim that will help contain the drippings. Spray the oven racks lightly with nonstick cooking spray. Arrange the slices directly on the racks, spacing them about ¼ inch (6 mm) apart. Set the oven temperature to 170°F (77°C). Use a folded kitchen towel to prop the oven door open by just under 1 inch (2.5 cm), to allow the moisture to escape. Let the meat dry for 2 hours. Turn the slices and continue to dry them for 1–2 hours more. When the meat is done, it should be firm and dry but still flexible.

Store the jerky in a resealable bag in the refrigerator, inspecting the meat frequently. Because the center of the jerky dries more slowly than the exterior, you may see wet spots within the first few days after the meat was dried. If you do, open the bag and leave it in direct sunlight for 1 hour or so to finish drying. The jerky will keep for up to 6 weeks.

Eye of round, top round, or bottom round beef, 3 lb (1.5 kg), trimmed of all exterior fat

Soy sauce, ⅔ cup (5 fl oz/160 ml)

Angostura or orange bitters, ⅓ cup (3 fl oz/80 ml)

Liquid smoke, 2 teaspoons (optional)

Hot pepper sauce, 1-2 teaspoons

Freshly ground pepper, 1 teaspoon

Garlic powder, 1 teaspoon

Onion powder, 1 teaspoon

Nonstick cooking spray

MAKES ABOUT 1 LB (500 G)

SALT-CURED BACON

A GAS GRILL, A HANDFUL OF WOOD CHIPS, AND A FOIL ROASTING PAN ARE ALL YOU NEED TO REACH BACON NIRVANA. THIS RECIPE CALLS FOR PINK CURING SALT #1, WHICH HELPS PRESERVE THE BACON AND ITS ICONIC PINK COLOR. LOOK FOR THE CURING SALT IN SPECIALTY FOOD SHOPS OR ONLINE.

Brown sugar, 3 tablespoons

Garlic, 1 tablespoon
finely chopped

Kosher salt, 4¾ teaspoons

Black pepper, 2 tablespoons
coarsely ground

Ground cinnamon, 1 teaspoon

Pink curing salt #1, 1 teaspoon

Ground cloves, ½ teaspoon

Pork belly, 2½ pounds
(1.25 kg), in a single piece

Disposable foil roasting pan, 1

Apple or maple wood
smoking chips, 3 cups
(18 oz/555 g)

Warm water, 4 cups
(32 fl oz/1 l)

MAKES ABOUT 2¼ POUNDS
(1.1 KG)

In a small bowl, combine the brown sugar, garlic, kosher salt, pepper, cinnamon, curing salt, and cloves and stir to combine. Rub the sugar mixture evenly over the pork belly, then put the meat in a large resealable plastic bag. Refrigerate the pork for 7 days, turning the bag over each day to coat the meat evenly with the cure.

Scrape the spice mixture off of the pork, rinse the pork, and pat dry. Place the meat on a roasting rack set in a disposable 12-by-10-inch (30-by-25-cm) aluminum foil roasting pan. Let the meat sit at room temperature while the grill heats.

Put 3 to 4 large handfuls of wood chips in a smoker box. Alternatively, form a double layer of foil into a packet, seal the chips snugly in the packet, and poke 5 holes in the top of the packet to vent smoke.

Place the smoking box or foil packet directly on one of the burner shields of a gas grill. Heat the grill for low-indirect cooking (one burner on, one burner off), adjusting the burner to maintain 200°F (95°C). When the wood chips begin to smolder, place the foil roasting pan setup on top of the cool side of the grill. Pour the warm water into the bottom of the pan. Close the lid and smoke the meat until an instant-read thermometer inserted into the thickest part of the meat registers 150°F (65°C), 2 to 2½ hours. You may need to prop the grill open slightly from time to time to keep the temperature around 200°F (95°C). If the temperature goes much higher than 225°F (110°C), the fat will begin to melt and you'll be cooking, not smoking, the meat.

Transfer the bacon to the refrigerator and let cool completely before slicing. To store, put into a resealable plastic bag and refrigerate for up to 2 weeks or freeze for up to 3 months.

TEA-SMOKED TROUT

THERE'S NO NEED TO INVEST IN A PRICEY OUTDOOR SMOKER TO MAKE YOUR OWN SMOKED FISH. A CARBON-STEEL WOK, A ROUND COOLING RACK, AND YOUR STOVE TOP WILL DO THE JOB. A MIXTURE OF JASMINE RICE AND LOOSE-LEAF GREEN TEA ADDS A SUBTLE HERBAL NOTE TO THE FISH.

Working from the cavity side, cut the fish in half lengthwise down the center, leaving the spine and bones attached to the fillets. Rub the fleshy side of the fish with 1 tablespoon of the sugar and the salt and pepper. Set aside for 10 minutes.

Set a round stainless-steel cooling rack to fit inside a carbon-steel wok (do not use a nonstick wok) and sits at least 2 inches (5 cm) above the bottom. Pat the fillets dry with paper towels and place them, skin side down, on the prepared rack. Line the wok with a sheet of aluminum foil long enough to extend beyond the rim by at least 4 inches (10 cm). Cut a second sheet of foil the same length and place it at a 90-degree angle to the first sheet. Mix together the rice and tea in the bottom of the wok, form into a pile, and sprinkle it with the remaining 1 tablespoon sugar. Cut a small disk of foil and place it over the rice mixture to form a barrier between the fish and the smoking material. This will prevent the fish from tasting overly smoked.

Turn on an exhaust fan and open a window. Cover the wok with a domed lid and place it over medium heat. When the rice mixture begins to send up a few wisps of smoke (after about 4 minutes), place the rack holding the fish in the wok, re-cover the wok, and fold the foil flaps up over the edges of the lid to seal in the smoke.

Reduce the heat to low and smoke the fish for 15 minutes. Uncover and cut into the thickest part of a fillet with a paring knife; the fish should be moist but no longer translucent. If the fish is not done, re-cover and continue to smoke for a few minutes more.

Uncover the wok and transfer the fish to a plate. Carefully lift the spine and bones from the fillets and discard. Serve the trout warm or refrigerate uncovered until cool. The trout will keep in an airtight container in the refrigerator for up to 1 week.

Trout, one 12–14 oz (375–440 g), cleaned and head removed

Brown sugar, 2 tablespoons

Sea salt, 1 teaspoon

Freshly ground pepper, ¼ teaspoon

Uncooked jasmine rice, ¼ cup (1¾ oz/50 g)

Loose-leaf green tea, ¾ teaspoon

MAKES 2 FILLETS;
SERVES 4–6 WITH CRACKERS

AQUAVIT & DILL-CURED LOX

LOX IS SALMON THAT HAS BEEN CURED WITH SUGAR, SALT, AND SOMETIMES
AQUAVIT, A STRONG CARAWAY-INFUSED LIQUOR. ALTHOUGH BEST KNOWN AS A
BAGEL TOPPING, LOX IS ALSO LOVELY ADDED TO SCRAMBLED EGGS AND SALADS,
TOSSED WITH PASTA AND LEMON, OR SERVED AS AN ELEGANT APPETIZER.

Wild salmon fillet with skin,
1 pound (500 g) (see note)

Aquavit, 2 tablespoons

Sea salt, 3 tablespoons

Sugar, 3 tablespoons

White pepper, 1 teaspoon,
coarsely ground

Fresh dill, ½ cup (¾ oz/20 g)
roughly chopped

**MAKES ¾ LB (375 G)
CURED FISH; SERVES 6–8**

*Note: Because lox is essentially
raw fish, be sure to shop for the
salmon at a reputable source and
buy fish that has been previously
frozen and stored at -4°F (-20°C)
for 7 days. The deep freeze is
necessary to kill any parasites.*

Place the salmon, skin side down, on a cutting board. With a pair
of fish tweezers or needle-nose pliers, gently tug the pin bones
free of the flesh, working in the direction in which they are angled.
With a sharp knife, cut the fillet in half crosswise.

Sprinkle the fleshy side of both salmon pieces evenly with the aquavit
and then sprinkle evenly with the salt, sugar, and pepper. Spread
the dill on 1 piece of the salmon and place the second piece, flesh
side down, on top. Wrap the stacked salmon tightly in a few layers
of plastic wrap and place on a dinner plate with a lip. Place a clean
cutting board or a few heavy plates on top of the fish to weigh it down.
Marinate the salmon in the refrigerator for 2 to 3 days, turning the
package over once or twice to distribute evenly the now-liquid brine.

Unwrap the salmon and wipe off most of the brine and seasoning.
To serve, place the salmon on a clean cutting board and, using a sharp,
thin-bladed knife positioned at a 45-degree angle, cut the salmon
into very thin slices, freeing the salmon from the skin as you slice.
Wrap the unsliced portion in plastic wrap and refrigerate for 5 days
or freeze for up to 3 months.

SWEETS
& SPREADS

AMARETTO ALMOND BUTTER

THIS EXTRA-RICH, VANILLA-SCENTED ALMOND BUTTER IS DIVINE SPREAD ON
APPLE SLICES, TOASTED BRIOCHE, OR HOMEMADE GRAHAM CRACKERS (PAGE 84).
THE RECIPE CAN BE EASILY DOUBLED, SO WHY NOT MAKE A BIG BATCH AND
GIVE SOME AS GIFTS IN HOMEY LITTLE JARS TIED WITH A RIBBON?

Preheat the oven to 350°F (180°C). Spread the nuts on a rimmed
baking sheet and bake, stirring once, until lightly toasted, about
10 minutes. Let the nuts cool to room temperature.

Transfer the nuts to a food processor. Add the sugar, oil, and salt and
pulse just until the nuts are coarsely ground, about 20 short pulses.
Using a sharp paring knife, split the vanilla bean lengthwise and
scrape the seeds out of the pod halves into the nut mixture. Process
the mixture continuously until it's creamy and smooth, 4–5 minutes.

Store the nut butter in an airtight container at room temperature for
up to 2 weeks, or refrigerate for up to 2 months, then bring to room
temperature before serving.

Whole almonds, 2 cups
(11 oz/345 g)

Light brown sugar,
¼ cup (2 oz/60 g) packed

Coconut oil, 1 tablespoon

Sea salt, ¼ teaspoon

Vanilla bean, 1

**MAKES 1 HEAPING CUP
(10 OZ/300 G)**

CLASSIC APPLE BUTTER

TRADITIONAL RECIPES LIKE THIS ONE COME IN HANDY DURING APPLE-PICKING SEASON. AS THE MIXTURE SLOWLY COOKS DOWN, THE SUGAR CARAMELIZES AND THE APPLE BUTTER TURNS A DEEP GOLDEN BROWN. BE SURE TO KEEP AN EYE ON THE BUTTER AS IT COOKS TO AVOID SCORCHING.

Sweet apples, such as Fuji, Gala, Empire, or Pink Lady, 4 lb (2 kg)

Apple cider, 1½ cups (12 fl oz/375 ml)

Juice of 1 lemon

Sugar, 2 cups (16 oz/500 g)

Ground cinnamon, 2 teaspoons

Ground cloves, ½ teaspoon

MAKES 5 HALF-PINT (8-FL OZ/250-ML) JARS

Have ready 5 sterilized jars and their lids.

Peel, quarter, and core the apples. In a large, nonreactive saucepan, combine the apples, cider, and lemon juice. Add ½ cup (4 fl oz/125 ml) water and bring to a boil over medium-high heat. Reduce the heat to low, cover, and simmer, stirring occasionally, until the apples are soft, about 30 minutes.

Working in batches if necessary, transfer the apple mixture to a food processor and purée just until smooth. Return to the saucepan and stir in the sugar, cinnamon, and cloves. Place over medium-low heat and cook uncovered, stirring frequently and scraping down the sides of the pan as needed, until the butter is thick and mounds on a spoon, about 1 hour.

Ladle the hot butter into the jars, leaving ¼ inch (6 mm) of headspace. Slide a metal chopstick or other thin tool down the side of each jar, between the glass and the butter, four or five times. This will release any air bubbles. Adjust the headspace, if necessary, then wipe the rim of each jar clean and seal tightly with a lid.

Store the jars in the refrigerator for up to 2 months.

ROASTED MAPLE SQUASH BUTTER

STORE-BOUGHT VERSIONS OF THIS AUTUMNAL TREAT ARE OFTEN TOO SWEET AND COME WITH A HEFTY PRICE TAG. HERE, THE COZY FLAVOR OF ROASTED WINTER SQUASH IS INTENSIFIED WITH CHAI SPICES AND A BIG SPLASH OF RUM. SERVE IT WITH SCONES OR PANCAKES OR SWIRLED IN VANILLA ICE CREAM.

Preheat the oven to 425°F (220°C). Line a rimmed baking sheet with parchment paper.

Halve the pumpkin, then scrape out the seeds and strings and discard. Cut the pumpkin into wedges, peel the wedges with a sharp vegetable peeler, and then cut into 2-inch (5-cm) chunks. Put the pumpkin chunks on the prepared baking sheet, drizzle with the oil, sprinkle with the salt, and toss to coat the pumpkin evenly. Spread the pumpkin in an even layer on the prepared baking sheet.

Roast the pumpkin until it can be easily pierced with a fork, 25–30 minutes. Drizzle the maple syrup over the pumpkin, toss to coat evenly, and continue to bake until the pumpkin is lightly caramelized and very tender, 15–20 minutes.

Let the pumpkin cool for about 15 minutes, then transfer to a food processor and process until smooth. You should have about 4 cups (2 lb/1 kg) purée. Transfer the purée to a heavy nonreactive pot and add the sugar, rum, cinnamon, nutmeg, and cardamom. Place over medium-low heat and bring to a gentle simmer. Reduce the heat to low and cook, stirring frequently, until the mixture is very thick, 30–40 minutes.

Ladle the mixture into containers with tight-fitting lids and let cool completely. Cover and refrigerate for up to 1 month or freeze for up to 3 months.

Sugar pumpkin or other winter squash, 1 small, about 4 lb (2 kg)

Canola oil, 1 tablespoon

Sea salt, ½ teaspoon

Grade A maple syrup, ¼ cup (3 fl oz/85 g)

Brown sugar, ¾ cup (6 oz/185 g) lightly packed

Spiced rum, 2 tablespoons

Ground cinnamon, 1 teaspoon

Nutmeg, ¼ teaspoon freshly grated

Ground cardamom, ¼ teaspoon

MAKES ABOUT 3 CUPS (30 OZ/900 G)

CHOCOLATE HAZELNUT SPREAD

UNLIKE ITS POPULAR COMMERCIAL COUNTERPART THAT LISTS SUGAR AND PALM OIL AS PRIMARY INGREDIENTS, THIS ALL-NATURAL CHOCOLATE HAZELNUT BUTTER IS PRIMARILY ROASTED HAZELNUTS AND COCOA POWDER. TRY IT ON CREPES, SMEAR IT ON TOAST, OR MELT IT AND SERVE IT OVER ICE CREAM.

Whole hazelnuts, 1 cup
(5 oz/150 g)

Hazelnut or walnut oil,
3 tablespoons

Vanilla extract, 1 teaspoon

Confectioners' sugar,
½ cup (2 oz/65 g)

Unsweetened cocoa powder,
¼ cup (¾ oz/20 g)

Salt, ¼ teaspoon

**MAKES ABOUT 1 CUP
(10 OZ/300 G)**

Preheat the oven to 350°F (180°C). Spread the hazelnuts on a rimmed baking sheet and toast until the nuts are golden brown and the skins are blistered, about 15 minutes. Working in small batches, rub the still-warm nuts vigorously between your palms to remove their papery skins. Do not worry if some skin remains intact.

Transfer the nuts to a food processor and process until they break down into a semiliquid paste, about 3 minutes. Add the oil and vanilla and process until smooth. Scrape the nut butter into a bowl.

Sift together the confectioners' sugar, cocoa powder, and salt into the nut butter, then stir together with a rubber spatula until completely blended.

Store the spread in a glass jar or other airtight container at room temperature for up to 1 week, or refrigerate for up to 1 month, then bring to room temperature before serving.

PEAR-CARDAMOM BUTTER

THIS SWEET SPREAD, INFUSED WITH A HINT OF CARDAMOM, IS SMOOTH AND
DELICATE. THE ADDITION OF ORANGE JUICE AND CITRUS ZEST TEMPERS THE
SWEETNESS OF THE PEARS. SPOON ON TOASTED BRIOCHE IN THE MORNING,
OR PAIR IT WITH A TANGY SHEEP'S MILK CHEESE OR A WEDGE OF BLUE CHEESE.

**Pears, preferably Bartlett,
4 lb (2 kg)**

**Fresh lemon juice,
2 tablespoons**

Sugar, 1½ cups (12 oz/375 g)

**Fresh orange juice, ¼ cup
(2 fl oz/60 ml)**

**Orange zest strips, 2,
each about 1 inch (2.5 cm)
wide and 4 inches (10 cm)
long and studded
with 2 whole cloves**

**Lemon zest strips, 2,
each about ½ inch (12 mm)
wide and 1 inch (2.5 cm) long**

Ground cardamom, 1 teaspoon

**Vanilla extract,
½ teaspoon**

**MAKES 6 HALF-PINT
(8-FL OZ/250-ML) JARS**

Have ready 6 sterilized jars and their lids.

Quarter and core the pears. In a large, nonreactive saucepan, combine the pears and lemon juice and toss to coat the pears evenly. Add ½ cup (4 fl oz/125 ml) water and bring to a boil over high heat. Reduce the heat to medium-low, cover, and simmer, stirring once or twice, until the pears are tender, about 20 minutes. Remove from the heat and let cool slightly.

Working in batches if necessary, pass the pears through a food mill or fine-mesh sieve set over a bowl. Transfer to a food processor and purée just until smooth. Return to the saucepan and stir in the sugar, orange juice, orange and lemon zest, cardamom, and vanilla. Bring to a boil over medium-high heat, reduce the heat to medium, and simmer uncovered, stirring frequently and scraping down the sides of the pan as needed, until the butter is thick and mounds on a spoon, about 1 hour. Remove and discard the zest strips.

Ladle the hot butter into the jars, leaving ¼ inch (6 mm) of headspace. Slide a metal chopstick or other thin tool down the side of each jar, between the glass and the butter, four or five times. This will release any air bubbles. Adjust the headspace, if necessary, then wipe the rim of each jar clean and seal tightly with a lid.

Store the jars in the refrigerator for up to 2 months.

LEMON CURD

SMOOTH AND CREAMY, THIS BRIGHT-TASTING SPREAD IS BOTH SWEET AND TART. FOR AN EVEN TARTER FLAVOR, SUBSTITUTE THE MORE COMMON LISBON LEMON. THIS VERSATILE CURD IS PERFECT FOR FILLING TARTS OR SANDWICH COOKIES, SPREADING BETWEEN CAKE LAYERS, OR SLATHERING ON SCONES AT TEATIME.

In a bowl, whisk together the sugar, whole eggs, and egg yolks. In a saucepan over low heat, combine the butter and lemon juice and warm, stirring, until the butter melts. Add the egg mixture to the saucepan and cook, stirring constantly, until the mixture has thickened and coats the back of a wooden spoon, about 5 minutes.

Remove from the heat and transfer the curd to a small heatproof container. Cover with plastic wrap, pressing it onto the surface, and refrigerate until ready to serve. Let come to room temperature before using, then stir in the zest. The curd will keep in the refrigerator for up to 1 month.

Sugar, ¾ cup (6 oz/185 g)

Eggs, 2 large whole, plus 4 large egg yolks

Unsalted butter, ½ cup (4 oz/125 g) cold, cut into small pieces

Fresh Meyer lemon juice, ½ cup (4 fl oz/125 ml) plus 2 tablespoons

Meyer lemon zest, 2 teaspoons grated

MAKES ABOUT 1½ CUPS (12 OZ/375 G)

MEMBRILLO

ROSY-HUED QUINCE PASTE IS TRADITIONALLY SERVED IN SLIVERS ON TOP OF MANCHEGO CHEESE. IT IS COSTLY TO BUY BUT IS EASY TO MAKE IN A SLOW COOKER. LOOK FOR QUINCES IN LATE FALL AND EARLY WINTER IN GROCERY STORES AND AT FARMERS' MARKETS.

Peel, quarter, and core the quinces. Cut the flesh into 2-inch (5-cm) chunks, place in a large saucepan, and add cold water just to cover. Using a vegetable peeler, remove a lemon zest strip 4 inches (10 cm) long from the lemon and add it to the pan. Place the pan over medium-high heat, bring to a simmer, cover, and reduce the heat to low to maintain a gentle simmer. Cook until the fruit is very tender when pierced with a fork but not falling apart, 15–30 minutes; the timing will depend on the ripeness of the fruit.

Drain the fruit and run it through a food mill fitted with the medium disk or process it in a food processor until smooth. Measure the purée; you will need 4½ cups (2⅓ lb/2.1 kg).

Juice the lemon. Combine the quince purée, sugar, and 2 tablespoons of the lemon juice in a 6½-qt (6.5-l) slow cooker. Cover and cook on high, stirring every 30 minutes, until the mixture is rosy colored and thickened, about 3 hours. Remove the lid and continue to cook on high until the mixture is very thick and a wooden spoon scraped along the bottom creates a clear path for a few moments. This final cooking time should be about 1 hour. If you are not sure if the mixture is thick enough, dab a small amount of it on a plate and refrigerate for 10 minutes; if the mixture sets, it is ready.

Line the bottom and sides of a 9-by-13-inch (23-by-33-cm) baking pan with parchment paper. Pour the hot quince mixture into the pan and smooth the top with an offset spatula. Cool to room temperature then refrigerate uncovered until the mixture is firmly set, at least 4 hours or up to overnight.

Cut into 8–10 slabs, wrap individually in plastic wrap, and store in the refrigerator for up to 1 month or in the freezer for up to 3 months.

Quinces, 3 lb (1.5 kg) (about 4 large)

Lemon, 1

Sugar, 4 cups (2 lb/1 kg)

MAKES 8-10 SLABS OF MEMBRILLO; EACH SLAB SERVES 10

CHUNKY APPLESAUCE

THIS CHILDHOOD TREAT, WHICH WILL FILL YOUR HOME WITH THE SWEET AND COMFORTING SCENT OF COOKED APPLES, MAKES A DELICIOUS SNACK WHEN SPRINKLED WITH A PINCH OF CINNAMON AND IS GOOD SPOONED ATOP ROASTED PORK. IT CAN ALSO BE MIXED INTO CAKE BATTERS FOR ADDED MOISTURE.

Fuji or Braeburn apples, 4

Sugar, ¼ cup (2 oz/60 g)

Fresh lemon juice, 2 teaspoons

Pinch of kosher salt

MAKES 4-6 SERVINGS

Peel, quarter, core, and coarsely dice the apples. You should have about 4 cups (16 oz/500 g). Transfer to a saucepan, add the sugar, lemon juice, salt, and ¼ cup (2 fl oz/60 ml) water, and stir well. Place over medium-high heat, bring to a boil, reduce the heat to low, cover, and simmer until the apples are tender, about 30 minutes. If the apples begin to dry out before they are ready, add a little more water.

Uncover the pan and mash the apples lightly with a wooden spoon or a silicone spatula. Cook uncovered for 5 minutes to evaporate some of the excess moisture. The applesauce should be thick. Remove from the heat and serve warm or chilled.

GET CREATIVE: Use a mix of 2 pears and 2 apples, or use all pears. You can also scent the sauce with a pinch of ground cinnamon, or add ¼ cup (1 oz/30 g) fresh cranberries and increase the sugar to 1 cup (8 oz/250 g) to balance the tartness. For a savory sauce to pair with pork, add ½ teaspoon chopped fresh thyme and season with salt and freshly ground pepper.

ENERGY BARS

THESE HOMEMADE ENERGY BARS, UNLIKE THEIR CONVENIENT
BUT ARTIFICIAL-TASTING STORE-BOUGHT KIN, ARE TRULY DELICIOUS.
PACKED WITH TOASTED NUTS, DRIED FRUITS, AND SPICES, THEY'RE
REAL FOOD THAT WILL HELP KEEP HUNGER AT BAY FOR HOURS.

Preheat the oven to 350°F (180°C). Spread the almonds, walnuts, and oats on a rimmed baking sheet and bake until lightly toasted, about 8 minutes. Remove from the oven and let cool completely.

Place the apples, dates, vanilla, and lemon zest in a food processor and pulse until the mixture is well chopped and forms a ball, about 30 short pulses. Add the toasted nuts and oats, cinnamon, nutmeg, and salt and process until the nuts are finely ground and the mixture forms moist clumps when pressed together with your fingers, about 2 minutes.

Line a 9-by-5-inch (23-by-13-cm) loaf pan with plastic wrap, allowing it to overhang the sides of the pan. Press the nut mixture evenly into the prepared pan, cover with the overhanging plastic wrap, and refrigerate until the mixture is firm to the touch, about 2 hours.

Using the plastic wrap, lift the slab out of the pan. Using a sharp knife, cut the slab into 8 bars and wrap each bar individually in plastic wrap. Store the bars in the refrigerator for up to 1 month.

FOR CHOCOLATE-CHERRY-AMARETTO BARS: Omit the rolled oats. Increase the slivered blanched almonds to 1 cup (5 oz/155 g) and add ¼ cup (1½ oz/45 g) semisweet chocolate chips to the food processor along with the nuts. Substitute almond extract for the vanilla extract and dried cherries for the dried apples, and mix into the nut mixture just before it is pressed into the pan.

FOR CARROT CAKE BARS: Omit the dried apples. When toasting the nuts and oats, increase the oats to 6 tablespoons (1 oz/30 g) and add ½ cup (2 oz/60 g) unsweetened shredded coconut to the baking sheet. Increase the dates to 1¼ cups (7½ oz/235 g), add ½ cup (2 oz/60 g) coarsely grated carrots (squeezed dry with paper towels) to the processor with the dates, and substitute 1½ teaspoons grated orange zest for the lemon zest.

Slivered blanched almonds, ½ cup (2½ oz/75 g)

Walnuts, ½ cup (2 oz/60 g)

Old-fashioned rolled oats, ¼ cup (¾ oz/20 g)

Chopped dried apple slices, ¾ cup (2 oz/60 g) lightly packed

Pitted Medjool dates, ½ cup (3 oz/90 g)

Vanilla extract, 1 teaspoon

Lemon zest, 1 teaspoon grated

Ground cinnamon, 1½ teaspoons

Nutmeg, ½ teaspoon freshly grated

Salt, ¼ teaspoon

MAKES ABOUT 8 BARS

GRANOLA X 3

GRANOLA OFTEN GETS A BAD RAP FOR BEING TOO SWEET, TOO BLAND, OR TOO OLD FROM WEEKS SPENT IN A BULK BIN AT THE STORE. HERE ARE THREE EASY RECIPES FULL OF CRISPY CLUSTERS OF OATS, NUTS, PUFFED RICE, AND DRIED FRUIT—PROOF THAT GRANOLA DESERVES TO GET BACK ITS GOOD NAME.

FOR STRAWBERRY ALMOND GRANOLA:

Old-fashioned rolled oats, 2½ cups (7½ oz/220 g)

Sliced almonds, 1 cup (4 oz/120 g)

Puffed rice cereal, ½ cup (½ oz/10 g)

Brown sugar, ½ cup (2½ oz/75 g) lightly packed

Salt, ¾ teaspoon

Ground cinnamon, ¾ teaspoon

Nutmeg, ¼ teaspoon freshly grated

Coconut oil, canola oil, or melted butter, ½ cup (4 oz/125 ml)

Almond extract, 1 teaspoon

Large egg white, 1, beaten until frothy

Freeze-dried strawberries, 1 cup (3 oz/90 g)

MAKES ABOUT 6½ CUPS (37 OZ/1.25 KG)

Preheat the oven to 350ºF (180ºC). Line a rimmed baking sheet with parchment paper or a silicone baking mat.

In a large bowl, combine the oats, almonds, rice cereal, brown sugar, salt, cinnamon, and nutmeg and mix well. In a small bowl, whisk together the oil and almond extract. Pour the oil mixture over the oat mixture. Add the egg white and toss with a rubber spatula to combine.

Pour the mixture on the prepared baking sheet, spreading it into a single layer. Bake until the mixture is nicely toasted, about 35 minutes, rotating the pan back to front about halfway through baking. Watch carefully during the last 10 minutes to make sure the granola in the corners of the pan doesn't burn. Remove and let cool completely. Stir in the strawberries just before serving or storing. Store in an airtight container at room temperature for up to 1 month.

FOR BANANA WALNUT GRANOLA: Preheat the oven to 325ºF (165ºC). Substitute ½ cup (2 oz/60 g) unsweetened flaked coconut and 1 cup (4 oz/125 g) coarsely chopped walnuts for the almonds, 1 teaspoon rum extract for the almond extract, and 1 cup (3½ oz/105 g) banana chips, broken into pieces, for the strawberries.

FOR MAPLE PECAN GRANOLA: Substitute 1 cup (4 oz/125g) coarsely chopped pecans for the almonds, ½ cup (4 fl oz/125 ml) grade A maple syrup for the brown sugar, and 1 teaspoon vanilla extract for the almond extract. Add ½ teaspoon ground ginger to the oat mixture.

GRANOLA BARS

THESE CRISPY, YET SLIGHTLY CHEWY GRANOLA BARS ARE ENDLESSLY ADAPTABLE AS LONG AS YOU KEEP THE RATIO OF DRY TO WET INGREDIENTS THE SAME. TRY THE TWO VARIATIONS BELOW OR CREATE YOUR OWN GRANOLA BAR FLAVORS.

Preheat the oven to 350°F (180°C). Spread the hazelnuts on a rimmed baking sheet and toast until the nuts are golden brown and the skins are blistered, about 15 minutes. Working in small batches, rub the still-warm nuts vigorously between your palms to remove their papery skins. Do not worry if some skin remains intact. Leave the oven on.

Spray a 9-by-13-inch (23-by-33-cm) baking pan with cooking spray. In a food processor, combine the hazelnuts, wheat germ, cinnamon, and salt and pulse just until finely ground, about 20 short pulses. Transfer to a bowl, add the oats, cranberries, and pecans, and stir to combine.

In a small saucepan, combine the butter, sugar, peanut butter, and maple syrup over medium heat, bring to a simmer, and cook for 1 minute, stirring constantly. Pour the peanut butter mixture evenly over the oat mixture, stir to combine, and let cool for 5 minutes.

Add the egg whites to the granola mixture and stir well. Press the mixture into the prepared pan, packing it down with a rubber spatula. Bake until golden brown around the edges and no longer sticky to the touch, 20–25 minutes. Cut into 12 bars in the pan, then let cool for at least 1 hour. Wrap the bars individually in plastic wrap and store in an airtight container at room temperature for up to 10 days.

FOR PEANUT CHOCOLATE GRANOLA BARS: Substitute ¾ cup (3½ oz/105 g) unsalted roasted peanuts for the hazelnuts and omit the cranberries. Chill the oat mixture for 15 minutes before adding the egg whites and 1 cup (6 oz/185 g) semisweet chocolate chips.

FOR VERY NUTTY BARS: Substitute toasted almonds and toasted cashews for the hazelnuts and ¼ cup (1¼ oz/35 g) each hulled pumpkin seeds and sunflower seeds and 2 tablespoons flaxseeds for the pecans. Use coconut oil in place of the butter and almond butter in place of the peanut butter. Add the grated zest of 1 orange with the egg whites.

Hazelnuts, 1 cup (5 oz/155 g)

Nonstick cooking spray

Wheat germ, ½ cup (1½ oz/45 g)

Ground cinnamon, 1 teaspoon

Salt, ½ teaspoon

Old-fashioned rolled oats, 2½ cups (7½ oz/235 g)

Dried cranberries, 1 cup (4 oz/125 g)

Pecans, ½ cup (2 oz/60 g) chopped

Unsalted butter, ½ cup (4 oz/125 g), cut into pieces

Brown sugar, ½ cup (3½ oz/105 g) firmly packed

All-natural peanut butter, ½ cup (5 oz/155 g)

Maple syrup, ⅓ cup (3 fl oz/80 ml)

Large egg whites, 2, lightly beaten until frothy

MAKES ABOUT 12 BARS

GRAHAM CRACKERS

THESE ARE JUST LIKE THE GRAHAM CRACKERS YOU GREW UP WITH, BUT THEY ARE MADE MORE EXCITING WITH THE ADDITION OF NUTMEG, CLOVES, AND CARDAMOM. THE KEY IS TO ROLL THE DOUGH EVENLY AND THINLY. ELASTIC ROLLING-PIN GUIDES OR A KEEN EYE AND CAREFUL ROLLING DO THE TRICK.

Whole wheat flour, 1¼ cups (6½ oz/200 g)

All-purpose flour, 1 cup (5 oz/155 g), plus more for dusting

Dark brown sugar, ½ cup (3½ oz/105 g) packed

Ground cinnamon, 1 teaspoon

Baking powder, ½ teaspoon

Baking soda, ½ teaspoon

Sea salt, ½ teaspoon

Nutmeg, ¼ teaspoon freshly grated

Ground cloves, ⅛ teaspoon

Ground cardamom, ⅛ teaspoon

Cold unsalted butter, 6 tablespoons (3 oz/90 g), cut into ½-inch (12-mm) chunks

Whole milk, ⅓ cup (3 fl oz/80 ml)

Honey, ¼ cup (3 oz/90 g)

Vanilla extract, 1 teaspoon

Sugar, 2 tablespoons

MAKES ABOUT 60 CRACKERS

In a food processor, combine the flours, brown sugar, cinnamon, baking powder, baking soda, salt, nutmeg, cloves, and cardamom and pulse just until combined. Scatter the butter over the flour mixture and pulse until the mixture resembles coarse cornmeal, about 20 short pulses.

Transfer the mixture to a large bowl. In a small bowl, whisk together the milk, honey, and vanilla until the honey dissolves. Add the milk mixture to the flour mixture and stir with a wooden spoon until the mixture forms a ball. Knead the ball a few times. Divide the ball into 2 portions, flatten each portion into a rectangle ¼ inch (6 mm) thick, and wrap separately in plastic wrap. Refrigerate for at least 4 hours.

Preheat the oven to 325°F (165°C). Line 2 baking sheets with parchment paper or silicone baking mats. Take 1 rectangle of dough out of the refrigerator and let it sit for 5 minutes at room temperature. On a well-floured work surface, roll out the dough ¹⁄₁₆ inch (2 mm) thick. Add more flour to the work surface to prevent sticking, if necessary.

Using a pastry wheel, cut the dough into 2-by-3-inch (5-by-7.5-cm) rectangles. Rewrap and chill any remaining scraps for 30 minutes before rerolling. Transfer the rectangles to a baking sheet and prick them a few times with a fork. Sprinkle the tops with some of the sugar.

Bake until crisp and just starting to brown around the edges, 15–20 minutes (the timing will depend on how thin the dough is), rotating the pan back to front at the halfway point. Remove from the oven and immediately transfer the crackers to a cooling rack. While the first batch of crackers is baking, repeat the process with the second rectangle of dough and then with the scraps. Once cool, store the crackers in an airtight container at room temperature for up to 2 weeks.

FLEUR DE SEL CARAMELS

TALENTED BAKER AND CANDY EXPERT JAMI CURL OF ST. CUPCAKE BAKERY IN PORTLAND, OREGON, SHOWED ME HOW TO MAKE THESE WONDERFULLY BUTTERY CARAMELS. THESE CANDIES CAN BE TRICKY, BUT JAMI'S METHOD OF STARTING WITH CORN SYRUP MAKES THIS RECIPE NEARLY FOOLPROOF.

Line an 8-inch (20-cm) square baking pan with parchment paper and spray with cooking spray; set aside. Scrape the seeds from the vanilla bean, place the cream, vanilla seeds and pod, and sea salt in a small saucepan and warm over medium-low heat until hot to the touch. Remove the vanilla bean pod, reduce the heat to low, and keep warm.

Place the corn syrup in a large saucepan. Heat over medium heat, swirling the pan occasionally, until the syrup starts to bubble. Carefully add half of the sugar, taking care not to get any on the side of the pan. Stir the sugar into the corn syrup to moisten. Repeat with the remaining sugar. Brush the sides of the pan with a moistened pastry brush to dissolve sugar crystals that have crept up the sides of the pan.

Clip a candy thermometer to the side of the pan and bring the mixture to a boil over medium heat, swirling the pan occasionally (do not stir), until the mixture registers 340–345°F (170–174°C) or the mixture turns coppery-brown.

Immediately turn off the heat, add the warm cream and butter; the mixture will bubble up and give off very hot steam, so be very careful. Whisk vigorously until the caramel is uniform in color and the butter has melted completely, about 30 seconds.

Quickly pour the caramel into the prepared pan and let it sit uncovered for 10 minutes. Sprinkle with the fleur de sel, cover loosely, and let the caramel sit at room temperature until set, 6 to 12 hours.

Place a cutting board on top of the baking pan, invert the pan, and ease the caramel out of the pan. Discard the parchment paper and cut the caramel into 1–1¼-inch (2.5–3-cm) pieces. Wrap the caramels in parchment squares and store at room temperature for up to 2 weeks.

VARIATION: Add 1 orange-spice tea bag to the cream mixture. Discard before adding to the caramelized sugar.

Nonstick cooking spray

Vanilla bean, 1,
split lengthwise

Heavy cream, ½ cup
(4 fl oz/125 ml)

Good-quality fine sea salt,
½ teaspoon

Light corn syrup, ¾ cup
(7½ oz/235 g)

Granulated sugar, 2 cups
(16 oz/500 g)

Unsalted butter,
10 tablespoons (5 oz/150 g),
at room temperature

Fleur de Sel, for sprinkling

MAKES ABOUT 1 POUND (500 G)

VANILLA MARSHMALLOWS

THE MIRACLE OF HOMEMADE MARSHMALLOWS—THE AMAZING ALCHEMY OF
GELATIN AND HOT SUGAR SYRUP—IS A SIGHT TO BEHOLD. ONCE YOU MAKE THEM,
YOU'LL NEVER AGAIN WANT TO BUY THOSE JET-PUFFED MARSHMALLOWS IN
PLASTIC BAGS. SERVE IN MUGS OF HOT CHOCOLATE OR SANDWICHED IN S'MORES.

Cornstarch, ¼ cup (1 oz/30 g)

Confectioners' sugar, ½ cup
(2 oz/60 g)

Vegetable oil, for oiling

Unflavored gelatin,
1½ tablespoons

Kosher salt, ¼ teaspoon

Cream of tartar, ¼ teaspoon

Granulated sugar, 1¼ cups
(10 oz/315 g)

Light corn syrup, 1 tablespoon

Vanilla extract,
1 teaspoon

MAKES ONE 9-BY-11-INCH
(23-BY-28-CM) SHEET

In a bowl, sift together the cornstarch and confectioners' sugar. Line
a 9-by-11-inch (23-by-28-cm) baking pan with aluminum foil and
lightly oil the foil. Sift ¼ cup (1 oz/30 g) of the sugar mixture into
the pan and tilt to coat the bottom and sides. Leave any excess evenly
in the bottom.

Pour ½ cup (4 fl oz/125 ml) water into the bowl of a stand mixer.
Sprinkle the gelatin over the water, gently whisk together, then let
stand for 5 minutes to soften. Whisk in the salt and cream of tartar
and beat on high speed until fluffy, 2–3 minutes.

Put ½ cup (4 fl oz/125 ml) water into a saucepan. Stir in the granulated
sugar and corn syrup. Place over medium-high heat, bring to a boil,
and cook, without stirring, until the mixture turns pale tan, about
250°F (120°C) on a candy thermometer, or firm-ball stage.

With the mixer on medium speed, drizzle the hot sugar syrup into the
gelatin mixture, aiming it between the beater and the side of the bowl.
Increase the speed to high and whip the mixture until it is white and
thick, about 5 minutes. Add the vanilla and beat until the mixture
cools, about 20 minutes.

Pour the mixture into the prepared pan. Dip an offset spatula in
cold water and smooth the surface. Let stand until a skin forms on
the surface, about 1 hour. Dust with ¼ cup (1 oz/30 g) of the sugar
mixture and let rest overnight at cool room temperature.

Line a pan with parchment paper and dust with the remaining sugar
mixture. Dip a knife into sugar and cut out marshmallow squares.
Layer the squares in the pan, dusting with more of the sugar mixture.
Cover tightly and store at room temperature for up to 2 weeks.

FOR VARIATIONS: See page 154.

PEANUT CARAMEL CORN

THE SWEET TREAT KNOWN AS CRACKER JACK DEBUTED AT THE CHICAGO WORLD'S FAIR IN 1893 AND HAS BEEN A HIT EVER SINCE. HERE, THERE'S NO PRIZE INSIDE, BUT THE FRESH POPCORN, MOLASSES-LACED CARAMEL, AND ROASTED PEANUTS PROVIDE PLENTY OF FLAVOR TO MAKE UP FOR IT.

Preheat the oven to 250°F (120°C). Line a rimmed baking sheet with parchment paper or a silicone baking mat. Put the safflower oil and 3 popcorn kernels in a large soup pot, cover, and heat over medium-high heat until the kernels pop. Add the remaining kernels, cover, and cook, shaking the pan occasionally, until the popping has subsided, 1½–2 minutes. Pour the popcorn into a large bowl. Add the peanuts and set aside.

Wipe out the pot and add the brown sugar, butter, corn syrup, and molasses. Bring the mixture to a simmer over medium heat, and cook, stirring constantly, until the mixture registers 245°F (118°C) on a candy thermometer. Remove the pot from the heat, then immediately add the vanilla extract, salt, and baking soda and stir to combine. Quickly add the popcorn and peanuts and stir with a wooden spoon until evenly coated with the caramel.

Pour the mixture onto the prepared baking sheet and bake for 40 minutes, stirring once or twice. Allow the mixture to cool before breaking it into pieces. Store in an airtight container at room temperature for up to 4 days.

Safflower oil, 2 tablespoons

Popcorn kernels, ½ cup (3 oz/90 g)

Salted roasted peanuts, 1 cup (5 oz/155 g)

Dark brown sugar, ½ cup (3½ oz/105 g) firmly packed

Unsalted butter, 5 tablespoons (2½ oz/75 g), at room temperature

Light corn syrup, ⅓ cup (3½ oz/105 g)

Light molasses, 2 tablespoons

Vanilla extract, ½ teaspoon

Salt, ¼ teaspoon

Baking soda, ½ teaspoon

MAKES 13 CUPS (26 OZ/700 G)

LAYERED MINT CHOCOLATES

JUST LIKE THE STORE-BOUGHT CANDIES IN GREEN FOIL, THESE CHOCOLATE BITES MELT IN YOUR MOUTH WITH A BRIGHT MINT FINISH. BE SURE TO USE PEPPERMINT OIL, NOT PEPPERMINT EXTRACT, OR THE MELTED CHOCOLATE WILL SEIZE. LOOK FOR THE OIL IN SPECIALTY BAKING SHOPS OR ONLINE.

Unsalted butter, 4 tablespoons (2 oz/60 g), melted

Peppermint oil, ¾ teaspoon

Semisweet chocolate (at least 60% cocoa solids), 1 pound (500 g), chopped

White chocolate, 8 oz (240 g), chopped

Green food coloring (optional)

MAKES 35 BITE-SIZE CHOCOLATES

Transfer 2 tablespoons of the melted butter, avoiding the white foam on top and milky whey at the bottom, to a small bowl, add the peppermint oil, and set aside. Discard the remaining butter.

Line a 9-by-13-inch (23-by-33-cm) baking pan with parchment paper. Put the semisweet chocolate in a heatproof bowl placed over (but not touching) gently simmering water in a saucepan. Stir with a rubber spatula until the chocolate is mostly melted and an instant-read thermometer inserted into the chocolate registers 116°F (47°C). Remove the chocolate from the heat and stir until it cools to 105°F (40°C). Add 4 teaspoons of the butter mixture and stir until smooth. Pour half of the chocolate into the prepared baking pan and smooth with an offset spatula. Set aside the remaining melted chocolate. Refrigerate the pan until the chocolate just sets (the surface will take on a matte finish), about 10 minutes.

While the first layer sets, melt the white chocolate in a clean bowl over the simmering water until it is nearly smooth (a few chunks are okay). Remove the bowl from the heat and stir until the chocolate cools to 105°F (40°C). Add the remaining butter mixture and a few drops of the food coloring, if using, and stir until evenly incorporated. Pour the white chocolate over the set semisweet chocolate layer and smooth with an offset spatula. Refrigerate until the white chocolate is just set, about 10 minutes.

If the reserved semisweet chocolate is too thick to spread, heat it briefly over simmering water to no more than 105°F (40°C). Pour it over the set white chocolate layer, smooth it with an offset spatula, and return the pan to the refrigerator until just set, about 10 minutes.

As soon as the third layer has set, cut the chocolate into 35 pieces. Transfer the candies to an airtight container with parchment paper between the layers and store at cool room temperature for up to 2 weeks.

CANDIED ZEST

SUGAR-COATED CITRUS ZEST DRESSES UP NEARLY ANY DESSERT, BUT IT MAKES AN ESPECIALLY NICE SWEET-BITTER GARNISH FOR SIMPLY FLAVORED ICE CREAMS AND FRUIT SORBETS. IT'S ALSO A GOOD TOPPING FOR CITRUS-BASED DESSERTS OR CAN BE EATEN ALONE AS A CANDY.

Using a citrus zester, remove the zest from the citrus fruits in long, thin strips, being careful not to remove too much of the white pith along with the zest. Reserve the fruits for another use.

Bring a saucepan three-fourths full of water to a boil over high heat. Add the zest strips and boil for 4 minutes. Drain and rinse under cold water. Repeat this step once more, using fresh water; this removes the bitterness from any pith attached to the zest.

In a saucepan, combine 2 cups (16 oz/500 g) of the sugar, 1½ cups (12 fl oz/375 ml) water, and the prepared citrus zest. Bring to a simmer over medium-low heat and cook until the zest is soft and translucent, about 30 minutes. Let the zest cool to room temperature in the syrup.

Set a wire rack over a rimmed baking sheet. Using a slotted spoon or tongs, transfer the zest strips to the rack, then discard the syrup. Let the zest stand until it feels only slightly tacky to the touch, about 2 hours.

Spread the remaining 1 cup (8 oz/250 g) sugar in a shallow dish. Toss the zest in the sugar until all of the pieces are completely coated. Use right away, or transfer to an airtight container and store at room temperature for up to 5 days.

Citrus fruits, 3 large lemons, 4 limes, or 2 oranges

Sugar, 3 cups (1½ lb/750 g)

MAKES ABOUT 1 CUP (3 OZ/90 G)

RASPBERRY PÂTES DE FRUITS

THESE EASY-TO-MAKE FRUIT JELLIES GET THEIR GELATINOUS STRUCTURE AND PURE FRUIT TASTE FROM THE PECTIN IN THE APPLESAUCE AND JAM. YOU CAN USE YOUR OWN HOMEMADE JAM, BUT BE SURE IT HAS A THICK, SOLID CONSISTENCY, AS RUNNY JAM WILL YIELD PUDDLES RATHER THAN SQUARES.

Seedless raspberry jam, 1 jar (16 oz/500 g)

Unsweetened applesauce, ½ cup (4½ oz/140 g)

Sugar, 1¼ cups (10 oz/310 g)

Fresh lemon juice, ½ teaspoon

Chambord or other raspberry liqueur, 1 teaspoon

MAKES ABOUT 36 PIECES

Line the bottom and sides of an 8-inch (20-cm) square baking pan with parchment paper.

In a heavy saucepan, combine the jam, applesauce, and 1 cup (8 oz/ 250 g) of the sugar and bring to a rolling boil over medium-high heat, stirring constantly. Reduce the heat to medium-low and cook, stirring frequently with a long-handled wooden spoon, until the mixture registers 210°F (99°C) on a candy thermometer. It will remain at this temperature for about 10 minutes, so be patient and continue cooking and stirring until the mixture registers 240°F (115°C), or the soft-ball stage. Cook for 1 minute.

Remove the pan from the heat, stir in the lemon juice and liqueur, and pour the mixture into the prepared pan. Let the mixture stand at room temperature until set, about 2 hours.

Cut the set sheet into 1-inch (2.5-cm) squares. Put the remaining ¼ cup (2 oz/60 g) sugar in a shallow bowl and roll the squares in the sugar to coat on all sides. Store the squares between layers of parchment paper in an airtight container at room temperature for up to 2 weeks.

FOR ORANGE-GINGER PÂTES DE FRUITS: Substitute blood orange or Seville orange marmalade for the raspberry jam. Add 2 teaspoons peeled and finely grated fresh ginger to the jam, applesauce, and sugar. Omit the liqueur.

FOR STRAWBERRY-ROSE PÂTES DE FRUITS: Substitute strawberry jam for the raspberry jam. Add ½ teaspoon rose water to the jam with the lemon juice. Omit the liqueur.

SAUCES & CONDIMENTS

BUTTERMILK RANCH DRESSING

MUCH MORE DELICIOUS THAN ITS STORE-BOUGHT EQUIVALENT, THIS CLASSIC
DRESSING IS ALSO A BREEZE TO MAKE: JUST STIR TOGETHER FIVE INGREDIENTS
AND SEASON WITH SALT AND PEPPER. YOU CAN DRIZZLE IT ON A SALAD,
USE IT TO DRESS COLESLAW, OR SERVE IT AS A DIP FOR RAW VEGETABLES.

Mayonnaise, ¾ cup
(6 fl oz/180 ml)

Buttermilk, ½ cup
(4 fl oz/125 ml)

Sour cream, ¼ cup
(4 fl oz/125 ml)

Fresh flat-leaf parsley,
½ bunch, leaves and tender
stems finely chopped

Fresh chives, ½ bunch,
finely chopped

Salt and ground white pepper

MAKES ABOUT 1½ CUPS
(12 FL OZ/375 ML)

In a bowl, stir together the mayonnaise, buttermilk, and sour cream.
Stir in the parsley and chives and season with salt and pepper.
Use right away, or transfer to a jar, cover tightly, and store in the
refrigerator for up to 4 days.

BASIC MAYONNAISE

HOMEMADE MAYONNAISE IS RICHER AND CREAMIER THAN ITS COMMERCIAL COUNTERPART. THIS RECIPE CALLS FOR A FOOD PROCESSOR, BUT YOU CAN ALSO USE AN ELECTRIC MIXER OR A WHOLE LOT OF ELBOW GREASE. DO NOT MIX THE OIL INTO THE EGG MIXTURE TOO QUICKLY OR THE SAUCE WILL CURDLE.

Large egg yolk, 1

Fresh lemon juice, 1 tablespoon

Dijon mustard, 1 teaspoon

Salt and freshly ground pepper

Extra-virgin olive oil, ⅔ cup (5 fl oz/160 ml)

MAKES ABOUT ¾ CUP (6 FL OZ/180 ML)

In a food processor, combine the egg yolk, lemon juice, and mustard and season with salt and pepper. Process briefly to combine. With the processor running, add the oil in a thin, steady stream and continue to blend until the mixture has a thick, smooth consistency. Use right away, or cover and refrigerate for up to 2 days.

FOR PESTO MAYONNAISE: Stir 1 tablespoon Kale Pesto (page 117) into the finished mayonnaise. Use as a sandwich spread.

FOR LEMON-HERB MAYONNAISE: Stir the grated zest of ½ lemon and 2 teaspoons each minced fresh flat-leaf parsley, chives, and dill into the finished mayonnaise. Use as a dip or sauce for chilled seafood.

FOR TAHINI MAYONNAISE: Stir 1 clove minced garlic into the finished mayonnaise. A little at a time, whisk in 2 teaspoons tahini. Then whisk in ½ teaspoon ground cumin and 1 teaspoon warm water. Taste and adjust the seasoning.

FOR TARTAR SAUCE: Stir in ½ cup (4 oz/125 g) Cucumber Relish (see opposite page). Use as a dip or sauce for fish or shellfish.

FOR MELLOWER MAYONNAISE: The noticeable flavor of olive oil in this mayonnaise may not be desirable for all uses. For a milder, more versatile mayonnaise, replace the olive oil with canola oil.

CUCUMBER RELISH

THIS COOLING CUCUMBER CONDIMENT IS A GOOD MATCH FOR THE SPICY RUBS
AND FIERY SAUCES OF GRILL OR BARBECUE COOKERY. SERVE IT ALONGSIDE
JUST-OFF-THE-FIRE BEEF OR CHICKEN, OR STIR IT INTO YOGURT FOR A FRESH
TAKE ON CUCUMBER-YOGURT SAUCE.

Peel the cucumber and cut into slices ¼ inch (6 mm) thick.

In a bowl, combine the cucumber, shallot, onion, vinegar, and sugar.
Toss several times until the sugar dissolves completely and the
cucumber slices are evenly coated. Sprinkle the mint on top and
toss to coat. Refrigerate to let the flavors meld, 1–2 hours.

Just before serving, drain the cucumber relish through a fine-mesh
sieve, as the cucumber will release up to 1 cup (8 fl oz/250 ml) liquid.
Discard the liquid. Add the salt and pepper and stir to combine.

Use right away, or cover tightly and refrigerate for up to 1 week.

English cucumber, 1

**Shallot, 1, very thinly sliced
and rings separated**

Red onion, ½, thinly sliced

**Cider vinegar, ¼ cup
(2 fl oz/60 ml)**

Sugar, 1 tablespoon

**Fresh mint leaves,
6-8, minced**

Salt, 1 teaspoon

**Freshly ground pepper,
1 teaspoon**

**MAKES ABOUT 2 CUPS
(16 OZ/500 G)**

SRIRACHA CHILI SAUCE

FROM FOUR-STAR RESTAURANTS TO RAMEN SHOPS, THIS THAI-INSPIRED FIERY SAUCE IS EVERYWHERE. THIS VERSION CALLS FOR FISH SAUCE AND IS FERMENTED, WHICH RESULTS IN AN IRRESISTIBLE MIX OF HOT, SALTY, AND SWEET FLAVORS. USE IT ON TOFU, PIZZA, EGGS, IN AIOLI (PAGE 126), AND MORE.

Have ready 1 sterilized jar and its lid.

In a food processor, combine the chiles, garlic, sugar, and salt and pulse until the mixture is mostly smooth (some seeds and some pieces of flesh should still be visible). Pour the mixture into the jar, cover loosely with plastic wrap, and set aside to ferment at room temperature until tiny bubbles begin to form around the edges of the jar, 2–3 days.

Transfer the mixture to a blender, add the vinegar and fish sauce, and process until very smooth. Run the mixture through a medium-mesh sieve and transfer to a sterilized bottle or jar. Cover tightly and store in the refrigerator for up to 6 months.

Red Fresno chiles, ¾ lb
(375 g), thinly sliced

Garlic, 1 clove

Sugar, 2 tablespoons

Sea salt, 1 teaspoon

Rice vinegar, 2½ tablespoons

Fish sauce, 2 teaspoons

**MAKES ABOUT 1 CUP
(8 FL OZ/250 ML)**

CHIPOTLE KETCHUP

PAIRING CHIPOTLE CHILES AND TOMATOES YIELDS A PERFECTLY BALANCED ACCOMPANIMENT ESPECIALLY SUITED TO GRILLED MEATS SUCH AS HAMBURGER, FLANK OR SKIRT STEAK, OR PORK CHOPS. THE CHILES—JALAPEÑOS THAT HAVE BEEN DRIED IN A SMOKE-FILLED CHAMBER—HAVE A DEEP, SWEET FLAVOR.

Tomatoes, 4 lb (2 kg)

Olive oil, 2 tablespoons

Yellow onions, 2, coarsely chopped

Garlic, 4 cloves, crushed

Ground coriander, 1 teaspoon

Ground allspice, ½ teaspoon

Cider vinegar, ½ cup (4 fl oz/125 ml)

Light brown sugar, ⅔ cup (5 oz/155 g) firmly packed

Chipotle chiles in adobo sauce, 1 can (7 oz/220 g)

Salt

MAKES 6 HALF-PINT (8-FL OZ/250-ML) JARS

Have ready 6 sterilized jars and their lids.

Blanch, peel, and core the tomatoes, then cut into chunks. Set aside. In a large nonreactive saucepan over medium heat, warm the olive oil. Add the onions and cook, stirring often, until translucent, about 5 minutes. Add the garlic, coriander, and allspice and cook until fragrant, about 2 minutes longer. Add the tomatoes, vinegar, and brown sugar and cook, uncovered, stirring occasionally, until the tomatoes are tender, about 30 minutes.

Meanwhile, cut the chiles in half and remove some or all of the seeds, depending on how spicy you want the ketchup. Reserve the adobo sauce and chop the chiles. When the tomatoes are ready, stir in the chiles and ¼ cup (2 fl oz/60 ml) of the sauce. Let cool briefly.

Working in batches, transfer the tomato mixture to a blender and process until smooth. Return the puréed mixture to the pan and bring to a boil over high heat. Reduce the heat to medium-low and simmer, stirring often, until thickened, about 20 minutes. Season with salt.

Ladle the hot ketchup into the jars, leaving ¼ inch (6 mm) of headspace. Slide a metal chopstick or other thin tool down the side of each jar, between the glass and the ketchup, four or five times. This will release any air bubbles. Adjust the headspace, if necessary, then wipe the rim of each jar clean and seal tightly with a lid.

Store the jars in the refrigerator for up to 1 month.

CLASSIC KETCHUP

MAKE THIS KETCHUP WHEN TOMATOES ARE AT THEIR SUMMER BEST. SWEET, JUICY GARDEN-FRESH TOMATOES ARE REDUCED TO A GENTLY SPICED, LUSCIOUSLY THICK CONDIMENT. YOUR FAVORITE PURCHASED KETCHUP WILL NEVER TASTE THE SAME AFTER YOU SAMPLE THIS IRRESISTIBLE VERSION.

Have ready 6 sterilized jars and their lids.

Blanch, peel, and core the tomatoes, then cut into quarters. In a large nonreactive saucepan over medium-low heat, warm the olive oil. Add the onions and bell peppers and cook until tender, about 5 minutes. Add the tomatoes and cook until tender, about 30 minutes.

Meanwhile, place the garlic, cinnamon, celery seeds, allspice, cloves, peppercorns, and red pepper flakes on a square of cheesecloth, bring the corners together, and tie with kitchen string. In a small nonreactive saucepan, bring the vinegar and cheesecloth bag to a boil over medium-high heat, cover, and remove from the heat.

Pass the tomato mixture through a food mill fitted with the medium disk into a clean nonreactive saucepan. Discard the cheesecloth bag and pour all but ¼ cup (2 fl oz/60 ml) of the vinegar into the tomato mixture. Stir in the sugar and salt. Bring to a boil over high heat, reduce the heat to medium, and simmer, stirring often, until the mixture is reduced by more than half and mounds slightly on a spoon, 45–60 minutes. Taste and adjust the seasoning with salt, sugar, and the remaining vinegar.

Ladle the hot ketchup into the jars, leaving ¼ inch (6 mm) of headspace. Slide a metal chopstick or other thin tool down the side of each jar, between the glass and the ketchup, four or five times. This will release any air bubbles. Adjust the headspace, if necessary, then wipe the rim of each jar clean and seal tightly with a lid.

Store the jars in the refrigerator for up to 1 month.

Tomatoes, 12 lb (6 kg)

Olive oil, 1 tablespoon

Yellow onions, 3, coarsely chopped

Small red bell peppers, 3, seeded and coarsely chopped

Garlic, 4 cloves, lightly crushed

Cinnamon stick, 1, crushed

Celery seeds, 1 tablespoon

Whole allspice, 1½ teaspoons

Whole cloves, 1½ teaspoons

Peppercorns, ½ teaspoon

Red pepper flakes, ½ teaspoon

Cider vinegar, 1½ teaspoons

Sugar, 2 tablespoons

Salt, 1¼ teaspoons

MAKES 6 HALF-PINT (8-FL OZ/250-ML) JARS

CHUNKY SALSAS

MEXICAN CUISINE IS MEMORABLE LARGELY BECAUSE OF THE FRESHNESS OF THE INGREDIENTS, SO IT MAKES NO SENSE TO BUY JARRED SALSA WHEN YOU CAN EASILY MAKE OUTSTANDING SALSAS AT HOME. THESE TWO "GO-TO" RECIPES ARE POPULAR FAVORITES. FOR A THIRD CLASSIC SALSA, SEE PAGE 114.

FOR PICO DE GALLO:

White onion, ⅓ cup (2 oz/ 60 g) finely chopped

Fresh cilantro leaves, 3 tablespoons chopped

Red Fresno or serrano chile, 1 tablespoon finely chopped

Garlic, 1 small clove, chopped

Sea salt, ½ teaspoon

Ripe tomatoes, 1 lb (500 g), cored, seeded, and chopped

Fresh lime juice, 1½ teaspoons

FOR MANGO HABANERO SALSA:

Ripe mangoes, 2

Red onion, ¼ cup (1½ oz/45 g) finely chopped

Green onions, 2, including tender green tops, thinly sliced

Habanero chile, ½, finely chopped

Fresh orange juice, 1 tablespoon

Fresh lime juice, 1 tablespoon

Orange zest, 1 teaspoon grated

Sea salt and freshly ground pepper

EACH RECIPE MAKES ABOUT 2 CUPS (12 OZ/370 G)

FOR PICO DE GALLO: Using a mortar and pestle, mash together 3 tablespoons of the onion, the cilantro, chile, garlic, and salt until a paste forms. Transfer the paste to a bowl, add the remaining onion, the tomatoes, and lime juice, and stir with a spoon to mix well. Let stand at room temperature for 30 minutes before serving to allow the flavors to meld. The salsa will keep in an airtight container in the refrigerator for up to 4 days.

FOR MANGO HABANERO SALSA: Stand 1 mango on one of its narrow edges, with the stem end facing you. Then, using a large, sharp knife, cut down about ¾ inch (2 cm) to one side of the stem, so the knife barely grazes the side of the large central pit, to remove 1 mango "half." Repeat on the opposite side of the fruit. Using a paring knife, score the cut side of a mango half in a grid pattern, being careful not to cut through the skin. Press gently against the skin side to push the cubes upward, then cut across the bottom of the cubes to release them from the skin. Repeat with the remaining half, and then cube the remaining mango the same way.

In a bowl, combine the mangoes, red and green onions, chile, orange and lime juices, and orange zest and stir well, mashing some of the fruit on the side of the bowl with the spoon. Season with salt and pepper, then let stand at room temperature for 30 minutes before serving to allow the flavors to meld. The salsa will keep in an airtight container in the refrigerator for up to 1 week.

TOMATILLO JALAPEÑO SALSA

THIS TRADITIONAL GREEN SALSA IS FAIRLY MILD. IF YOU PREFER MORE HEAT, LEAVE THE SEEDS AND RIBS IN THE CHILE AND/OR ADD A SECOND CHILE. SERVE THE SALSA WITH TORTILLA CHIPS OR COMBINE IT WITH LIGHTLY FRIED TORTILLAS, SCRAMBLED EGGS, AND CHEESE TO MAKE CHILAQUILES.

Tomatillos, 1½ lb (750 g), husks removed

Jalapeño chile, 1, stem removed

Garlic, 4 large cloves, unpeeled

Olive oil, 2 teaspoons

Fresh cilantro leaves, ½ cup (½ oz/15 g), chopped

White onion, ½ cup (2½ oz/ 75 g), finely chopped

Lime juice, 2 tablespoons

Ground cumin, 1 tablespoon

Dark brown sugar, 1 teaspoon

Dried Mexican oregano, 1 teaspoon

Sea salt and freshly ground pepper

MAKES ABOUT 3 CUPS (1½ LB/750 G)

Position an oven rack 6 inches (15 cm) below the heat element and preheat the broiler. Line a rimmed baking sheet with aluminum foil.

Place the tomatillos, chile, and garlic on the prepared baking sheet, drizzle with the oil, and toss to coat evenly. Broil the vegetables, turning them as needed with tongs, until they are lightly charred and have begun to collapse, about 7 minutes for the garlic and chile and 10–12 minutes for the tomatillos. Remove from the oven and let cool until they can be handled.

With a paring knife, scrape the skin and some of the seeds from the chile, peel the garlic, and core the tomatillos. Transfer the tomatillos, chile, and garlic to a food processor and add the cilantro, onion, lime juice, cumin, brown sugar, and oregano. Pulse until all of the ingredients are well combined and a chunky salsa has formed. Transfer to a bowl and season with salt and pepper. Let stand at room temperature for 30 minutes before serving to allow the flavors to meld. The salsa will keep in an airtight container in the refrigerator for up to 2 weeks.

HARISSA

HARISSA IS A SPICY RED CHILE CONDIMENT FROM NORTH AFRICA THAT IS SERVED ALONGSIDE TAGINES (TRADITIONAL STEWS) AND OTHER DISHES. THIS HOMEMADE VERSION CAN ALSO BE USED AS A BASE FOR ENCHILADA SAUCE, A FLAVORING FOR CHILI, OR A RUB FOR GRILLED MEATS.

Put all of the chiles in a large heatproof bowl and pour the boiling water into the bowl. Top the chiles with a saucer to keep them submerged and let soak for 1 hour.

Put on a pair of rubber gloves to protect your skin from capsaicin, the active element in chiles that produces a burning sensation, then split the chiles open and swish them around in the soaking water to remove most of the seeds. Discard the soaking liquid and seeds.

In a food processor, combine the chiles, oil, lemon juice, garlic, caraway, mint, cumin, salt, and pepper and process until smooth, stopping to scrape down the sides of the processor bowl as needed. Transfer the chile mixture to a fine-mesh sieve placed over a bowl and press it through the sieve with a rubber spatula. Discard any solids left in the sieve.

Transfer the condiment to an airtight container and store in the refrigerator for up to 1 month.

Dried guajillo chiles, 8

Dried New Mexican chiles, 8

Boiling water, 8 cups (64 fl oz/2 l)

Extra-virgin olive oil, 3 tablespoons

Fresh lemon juice, 2 tablespoons

Garlic, 1 tablespoon finely chopped

Ground caraway, 1 teaspoon

Dried mint, 1 teaspoon

Ground cumin, ½ teaspoon

Sea salt, 1 teaspoon

Freshly ground pepper, ½ teaspoon

MAKES ABOUT 1¼ CUPS (10 FL OZ/310 ML)

KALE PESTO

HERE, THE BASIL TYPICALLY USED IN PESTO IS REPLACED WITH EARTHY KALE, WHICH GIVES THE SAUCE A BOLDER, SLIGHTLY SPICY FLAVOR. THIS CONDIMENT IS DELICIOUS MIXED WITH SCRAMBLED EGGS, SPREAD ON A SANDWICH OR PIZZA, WHISKED INTO SALAD DRESSING, OR SPOONED OVER GRILLED FISH.

With a food processor running, drop the garlic cloves through the feed tube. Turn off the processor, add the cheese and pine nuts, and pulse briefly. Add the kale, turn on the processor again, and pour the oil through the feed tube in a thin, steady stream, processing until a moderately thick paste forms. As you work, stop the processor occasionally and scrape down the sides of the bowl.

Transfer the pesto to a bowl, stir in the salt and pepper, and then taste the pesto. Add more cheese, salt, and/or pepper if needed to balance the flavors. Use the pesto right away, or top with a thin layer of oil (to prevent discoloration), cover, and store in the refrigerator for up to 1 week. Bring the pesto to room temperature and stir well before using.

Garlic, 2 cloves

Parmesan or pecorino romano cheese, ½ cup (2 oz/60 g), grated

Pine nuts, ¼ cup (1¼ oz/35 g), toasted

Kale leaves, 2 cups (2 oz/60 g) packed

Extra-virgin olive oil, ½ cup (4 fl oz/125 ml)

Salt, ¼ teaspoon

Freshly ground pepper, ⅛ teaspoon

MAKES ABOUT 1 CUP (8 OZ/250 G)

ROMESCO SAUCE

ROMESCO SAUCE, SPICY AND THICKENED WITH ALMONDS, IS A VERSATILE SPANISH CONDIMENT FOR MANY GRILLED FOODS, INCLUDING FISH AND VEGETABLES. SPOON IT ATOP FENNEL OR HALIBUT, SPREAD IT ON A SANDWICH, OR SERVE AS A FLAVORFUL DIP OR TOPPING FOR GRILLED BREAD.

Dried ñora, ancho, or pasilla chiles

Canola oil, for brushing

Red bell pepper, 1, quartered lengthwise and seeded

Plum tomatoes, 2, quartered and seeded

Yellow onion, 1, quartered

Garlic, 4 cloves

Slivered blanched almonds, ¼ cup (1 oz/30 g)

Sherry vinegar, 2 tablespoons

White wine, 2 tablespoons

Spanish smoked paprika, 2 teaspoons

Salt and freshly ground pepper

MAKES ABOUT 1 CUP (8 OZ/250 G)

In a bowl, combine the chiles and warm water to cover and let stand until soft and pliable, about 10 minutes. Remove the chiles from the soaking water, reserving the water. Pat the chiles dry, then halve and seed them.

Prepare a charcoal or gas grill for direct-heat grilling over medium-high heat. Brush a grilling basket with oil, then brush the chiles, bell pepper, tomatoes, onion, and garlic with oil.

When the fire is ready, arrange the vegetables in the grilling basket and place directly over the fire. Grill, turning the vegetables often, until lightly charred on all sides, about 5 minutes for the chiles, 8–10 minutes for the bell pepper, 6–8 minutes for the tomatoes, 8–10 minutes for the onion, and 2–3 minutes for the garlic. Transfer to a bowl, cover, and let steam for 10 minutes.

Using your fingers or a paring knife, peel the bell pepper and tomatoes and discard the skins. In a blender or food processor, combine the bell pepper, tomatoes, chiles, onion, garlic, almonds, vinegar, wine, and paprika and process until a pourable sauce forms, adding the reserved soaking water from the chiles as needed to achieve a good consistency. Taste and adjust the seasoning with salt and pepper.

Serve right away, or transfer to an airtight container and store in the refrigerator for up to 1 week.

SAVORY SUNFLOWER SPREAD

SKEPTICS OF SAVORY SEED SPREADS WILL BE CONVERTED AFTER JUST ONE TASTE OF THIS UMAMI-RICH MIXTURE. LACED WITH HERBS AND CITRUS, IT IS A GREAT ADDITION TO A LUNCH-BOX SANDWICH AND MAKES AN ELEGANT DIP WITH CRACKERS AND CRUDITÉS BEFORE A COMPANY DINNER.

Preheat the oven to 350°F (180°C). Spread the seeds on a rimmed baking sheet and bake until lightly toasted, 8–10 minutes.

Transfer the seeds to a food processor and add the lemon juice, garlic, parsley, rosemary, oregano, soy sauce, lemon zest, salt, sage, and pepper. Process, stopping to scrape down the sides of the bowl as needed, until the mixture is finely ground, about 2 minutes. With the processor running, slowly add the oil and process until smooth. If the mixture is too thick to spread, add water, 1 tablespoon at a time, until the mixture is a good consistency.

Serve right away, or transfer to an airtight container and store in the refrigerator for up to 2 weeks.

Raw sunflower seeds,
2 cups (3 oz/90 g), hulled

Fresh lemon juice,
⅓ cup (3 fl oz/80 ml)

Garlic, 1½ teaspoons
finely chopped

Fresh flat-leaf parsley,
2 tablespoons chopped

Fresh rosemary, 2 teaspoons
chopped

Fresh oregano, 2 teaspoons
chopped

Soy sauce, 2 teaspoons

Lemon zest, 1 teaspoon
grated

Fine sea salt, 1 teaspoon

Dried sage, ½ teaspoon

Freshly ground pepper,
¼ teaspoon

Extra-virgin olive oil, ⅓ cup
(3 fl oz/80 ml)

**MAKES ABOUT 1¼ CUPS
(12½ OZ/375 G)**

HORSERADISH X 2

JARRED HORSERADISH PALES ALONGSIDE THE AROMATIC BITE OF FRESHLY GRATED HORSERADISH. THERE ARE TWO OPTIONS FOR SAUCES: A CREAMY, ZESTY VERSION AND A MILDER, RED OR YELLOW BEET VERSION. LOOK FOR HORSERADISH ROOT THAT IS FIRM AND WITHOUT ANY GREENISH TINGE UNDER THE SKIN.

Red or yellow beets,
14 oz (440 g)

Fresh horseradish root,
3-inch (7.5-cm) piece,
about 2 oz (60 g), peeled

Red wine or cider vinegar,
2 tablespoons

Salt, ½ teaspoon

Sugar, ¼ teaspoon

MAKES ABOUT 1¾ CUP
(13½ OZ/425 G)

FOR BEET HORSERADISH: In a small saucepan, combine the beets with water to cover by 2 inches (5 cm) and bring to a boil over high heat. Reduce the heat to maintain a simmer and cook until a paring knife slips easily into the largest beet, about 40 minutes. Drain the beets and let cool until they can be handled, then slip off the skins.

Grate the beets on the fine holes of a box grater and transfer to a bowl. Grate the horseradish root on the same holes until you have ½ cup (4 oz/125 g) and add to the bowl. Add the vinegar, salt, and sugar and mix well. Let stand for 1 hour before serving to let the flavors meld. The horseradish will keep in an airtight container in the refrigerator for up to 3 weeks.

FOR CREAMY HORSERADISH: Follow the directions for beet horseradish but substitute 1 cup (8 fl oz/250 ml) crème fraîche or sour cream for the beets and 1 tablespoon white wine vinegar for red wine vinegar.

MOSTARDA DI FRUTTA

MOSTARDA, AN ITALIAN CONDIMENT OF CANDIED FRUIT IN MUSTARDY SYRUP, IS TYPICALLY SERVED ALONGSIDE BOILED MEATS AND SOMETIMES CREAMY CHEESES. JARS OF IMPORTED MOSTARDA ARE PRICEY, BUT THIS STREAMLINED VERSION, WHICH COOKS IN JUST 45 MINUTES, COSTS ONLY A FEW DOLLARS TO MAKE.

Underripe Bosc pear, 1 large, about ½ lb (250 g)

Quince or Granny Smith apple, 1 large, about ½ lb (250 g)

Dried apricots, ¼ lb (125 g), sliced

Dried figs, ¼ lb (125 g), quartered

Sugar, 1½ cups (12 oz/375 g)

White balsamic or white wine vinegar, 1 cup (8 fl oz/250 ml)

Orange, 1

Plums, ½ lb (250 g), pitted and cut into wedges ½ inch (12 mm) thick

Dry mustard, 1 tablespoon

MAKES ABOUT 2 ONE-PINT (16-FL OZ/500-ML) JARS

Have ready 2 sterilized jars and their lids.

Peel and core the pear and quince, then cut into ¾-inch (2-cm) chunks. In a large nonreactive pot, combine the pear, quince, apricots, figs, sugar, and vinegar. With a vegetable peeler, cut 2 zest strips each 4 inches (10 cm) long from the orange and add them to the pot. Reserve the orange for another use.

Bring the mixture to a simmer over medium-low heat. Reduce the heat to maintain a very gentle simmer and cook, stirring frequently, until the fruit is easily pierced with a fork, about 15 minutes. Add the plums and simmer until they are tender but not falling apart, about 10 minutes longer.

Using a slotted spoon, transfer the fruits to the prepared jars, leaving the syrup in the pot. Pour any juices that accumulate in the jars back into the pot.

Increase the heat to medium and simmer until the syrup is reduced by half, about 5 minutes. Whisk the dry mustard into the syrup and simmer for 1 minute. Ladle the hot syrup into the jars over the fruits. Let cool completely in the refrigerator, then screw the lids onto the jars and refrigerate for up to 2 weeks or freeze for up to 3 months.

BEER MUSTARD

MUSTARD HAS ALWAYS BEEN A FAVORITE CONDIMENT. ADD BEER AND IT'S EVEN BETTER. THE DARKER THE BEER, THE MORE INTENSE THE FLAVOR WILL BE. SERVE THIS MUSTARD CLASSICALLY, ON HOT DOGS, SAUSAGES, AND HAM, OR USE AS THE BASE OF A TANGY VINAIGRETTE.

In a glass or ceramic bowl, whisk together the dry mustard, beer, vinegar, and salt until smooth. Cover and let stand for at least 2 hours or for up to overnight.

Transfer the mixture to a nonreactive saucepan. Whisk in the sugar, mustard seeds, and egg, whisking constantly until the mixture reaches a full boil. The mustard should be amber-yellow and strongly flavored. Let cool. Use right away, or cover tightly and store in the refrigerator for up to 1 month.

Dry mustard, ½ cup
(1½ oz/45 g)

Amber or dark beer, ½ cup
(4 fl oz/125 ml)

Cider vinegar, 2 tablespoons

Salt, ½ teaspoon

Sugar, ¼ cup (2 oz/60 g)

Yellow mustard seeds,
1 tablespoon, toasted

Large egg, 1, beaten

**MAKES ABOUT ¾ CUP
(6 OZ/185 G)**

DIJON MUSTARD

THE FAMED MUSTARD ASSOCIATED WITH DIJON, FRANCE, IS EASY TO MAKE. SOME VERSIONS REQUIRE GRINDING WHOLE MUSTARD SEEDS AND SPICES. THIS ONE CHAMPIONS SIMPLICITY BY COMBINING DRY MUSTARD WITH A FEW ESSENTIAL INGREDIENTS. THE RESULT IS SMOOTH AND CREAMY, WITH A NICE SPICY HIT.

Have ready 2 sterilized jars and their lids.

In a bowl, stir together the mustard and ½ cup (4 fl oz/125 ml) water until smooth. Set aside.

In a small nonreactive saucepan, combine the wine, onion, and garlic and bring to a boil over high heat. Reduce the heat to medium, stir in the sugar and salt, and simmer uncovered, stirring often, until reduced by half, about 20 minutes.

Pour the wine mixture through a fine-mesh sieve placed over the bowl holding the mustard. Stir to mix well. Transfer the mustard to the saucepan and cook over medium heat, stirring frequently, until thickened, about 20 minutes.

Spoon the hot mustard into the jars, leaving ¼ inch (6 mm) of headspace. Slide a metal chopstick or other thin tool down the side of each jar, between the glass and the mustard, four or five times. This will release any air bubbles. Adjust the headspace, if necessary, then wipe the rim of each jar clean and seal tightly with a lid.

Store the jars in the refrigerator for up to 1 year. For the best flavor, let the mustard stand for at least 2 weeks before using.

FOR HONEY DIJON MUSTARD: Omit the sugar. Stir in 2 tablespoons honey before transferring the mustard to the jars.

FOR TARRAGON DIJON MUSTARD: Stir in 1 tablespoon chopped fresh tarragon before transferring the mustard to the jars.

FOR DIJON WITH MUSTARD SEEDS: Stir in 2 teaspoons brown mustard seeds during the last 5 minutes of cooking.

Dry mustard, 1⅓ cups (4 oz/125 g)

Dry white wine or flat Champagne, 2 cups (16 fl oz/500 ml)

Yellow onion, 1, chopped

Garlic, 3 cloves, finely chopped

Sugar, 2 teaspoons

Salt, 2 teaspoons

MAKES 2 HALF-PINT (8-FL OZ/250-ML) JARS

AIOLI X 2

HERE ARE TWO QUICK AND EASY FLAVORED MAYONNAISES. THE LEMON AIOLI
IS THE PERFECT ACCOMPANIMENT TO FRIED FISH, STEAMED ARTICHOKES,
AND ROASTED ASPARAGUS. THE RED PEPPER AIOLI PAIRS WELL WITH ROASTED
POTATOES, RED MEATS, GARLICKY GRILLED CHICKEN, AND CRAB CAKES.

FOR MEYER LEMON AIOLI:

Canola oil and olive oil,
¼ cup (2 fl oz/60 ml) each

Large egg yolks, 3

Dijon mustard, 1 tablespoon

Garlic, 3 cloves,
coarsely chopped

Salt, ½ teaspoon

Ground white pepper,
¼ teaspoon

Fresh Meyer lemon juice,
3–4 tablespoons

FOR RED PEPPER AIOLI:

Garlic, 6 cloves

Salted boiling water to cover

Olive oil, ½ cup (4 fl oz/120 ml)

Canola oil, ¼ cup
(2 fl oz/60 ml)

Large egg yolks, 2

Red bell pepper, 1, grilled,
peeled, seeded, and quartered

Sweet paprika and chile
powder, 1 teaspoon *each*

Salt and freshly ground
black pepper

Hot pepper sauce, 3–4 dashes

**EACH RECIPE MAKES ABOUT
2 CUPS (16 FL OZ/500 ML)**

FOR MEYER LEMON AIOLI: Pour the oils into a measuring cup
with a spout. In a blender or food processor, combine the egg yolks,
mustard, garlic, salt, and white pepper. Pulse several times until the
garlic is pulverized. With the motor running, add the oils in a slow,
steady stream. Stir in 3 tablespoons of the lemon juice, then stir in
the remaining 1 tablespoon lemon juice if needed to thin the aioli;
it should be the consistency of mayonnaise. Taste and adjust the
seasoning. Spoon into a serving bowl, cover, and refrigerate until
serving. It will keep for up to 1 week.

FOR RED PEPPER AIOLI: Place the garlic in a small heatproof
bowl. Add boiling salted water to cover and let stand for 1 minute.
Drain the garlic and pat dry; reserve ¼ cup (2 fl oz/60 ml) of the
blanching liquid.

Pour the oils into a measuring cup with a spout. In a blender, combine
the garlic, egg yolks, red pepper, paprika, chile powder, 1 teaspoon
salt, ½ teaspoon black pepper, and hot pepper sauce. Blend until
the garlic and red pepper are pulverized. With the motor running,
add the oils in a slow, steady steam. Stir in the reserved garlic
blanching liquid, 1 tablespoon at a time, as needed to thin the aioli;
it should be the consistency of mayonnaise. Taste and adjust the
seasoning. Spoon into a serving bowl, cover, and refrigerate until
serving. It will keep for up to 1 week.

CLASSIC OLIVE TAPENADE

THIS TIME-HONORED PASTE OF OLIVES, CAPERS, ANCHOVIES, AND GARLIC HAILS FROM PROVENCE, WHERE OLIVE TREES AND CAPER BUSHES FLOURISH IN THE SUNNY CLIMATE. IT'S A DELICIOUS SPREAD FOR GRILLED BREAD OR PIZZA, DIP FOR CRUDITÉS, OR RELISH FOR GRILLED LAMB, FISH, OR VEGETABLES.

In a food processor, combine the olives, capers, anchovy, garlic, lemon zest, pepper, and 2 tablespoons olive oil. Pulse to form a coarse purée, adding more oil if needed for spreadability.

Transfer the tapenade to a bowl and use right away, or cover and refrigerate for up to 5 days, then bring to room temperature before using.

Pitted Niçoise or Kalamata olives, ½ cup (2½ oz/75 g)

Capers, 1 tablespoon, rinsed

Anchovy fillet, 2 teaspoons, chopped

Garlic, 1 teaspoon minced

Lemon zest, 1 teaspoon grated

Freshly ground pepper, ½ teaspoon

Fruity extra-virgin olive oil, 2-3 tablespoons

MAKES ABOUT ¾ CUP (6 OZ/185 G)

GREEN OLIVE RELISH

UNLIKE MANY STORE-BOUGHT RELISHES, WHICH LACK BOLD TASTE AND TEXTURE, THIS TANGY, SALTY VERSION IS FULL OF COLOR, FLAVOR, AND A NICE TEXTURAL CONTRAST BETWEEN THE SOFT, BRINY OLIVES AND THE STURDY, TART LEMON PEEL. SERVE WITH ROASTED MEATS OR AS THE CENTERPIECE OF A CHEESE PLATE.

Meyer lemons, 2, quartered lengthwise and seeded

Shallot, 1, coarsely chopped

Fresh flat-leaf parsley, 2 tablespoons finely chopped

Pitted green olives, ½ cup (2½ oz/75 g)

Coriander seeds, 1 teaspoon

White balsamic vinegar, 1 teaspoon

Sea salt, ¼ teaspoon

Ground white pepper, ¼ teaspoon

MAKES ABOUT 1 CUP (8 OZ/250 G)

Scoop out about half of the pulp from each lemon quarter and discard. Coarsely chop the lemon quarters and put them in a food processor or blender. Add the shallot, parsley, and olives and pulse several times until minced but not puréed. Transfer to a bowl and stir in the coriander seeds and vinegar. Season with the salt and pepper. For a chunkier relish, chop the olives coarsely by hand and stir them into the minced lemon mixture with the coriander and vinegar.

Serve right away, or cover and refrigerate for up to 3 days, then bring to room temperature before serving.

APPLE-ONION CHUTNEY

ANY APPLE VARIETY WORKS WELL IN THIS TRADITIONAL ENGLISH CHUTNEY,
ALTHOUGH GOOD BAKING APPLES, SUCH AS GRANNY SMITH AND PIPPIN,
THAT HOLD THEIR SHAPE WHEN COOKED, ENSURE A CHUNKIER CHUTNEY.
SERVE AS AN ACCOMPANIMENT TO ROAST PORK LOIN OR ROAST BEEF.

Have ready 4 sterilized jars and their lids.

In a nonreactive saucepan, combine the raisins, vinegar, brown sugar, zest strips, and cloves. Add 2½ cups (20 fl oz/625 ml) water and stir to mix well. Bring to a boil over high heat. Remove from the heat and set aside.

In a large nonreactive saucepan over medium-low heat, melt the butter with the olive oil. Add the onions and cook, stirring occasionally, until tender, about 15 minutes. Add the raisin mixture and the apples and bring to a boil over high heat. Reduce the heat to medium-low and simmer uncovered, stirring occasionally, until the apples are just tender, about 25 minutes. Add the mint and thyme and continue to cook until the apples are tender, about 5 minutes longer. Discard the zest strips.

Ladle the hot chutney into the jars, leaving ¼ inch (6 mm) of headspace and using a small rubber spatula to push the apple and onion pieces gently into the jar so that they are covered with liquid. Slide a metal chopstick or other thin tool down the side of each jar, between the glass and the chutney, four or five times. This will release any air bubbles. Adjust the headspace, if necessary, then wipe the rim of each jar clean and seal tightly with a lid.

Store the jars in the refrigerator for up to 2 weeks.

Raisins, 2 cups (12 oz/375 g)

Cider vinegar, 1 cup
(8 fl oz/250 ml)

Light brown sugar, 1 cup
(7 oz/220 g) firmly packed

Lemon zest strips, 4, each
½ inch (12 mm) wide and
2 inches (5 cm) long

Ground cloves, ½ teaspoon

Unsalted butter,
2 tablespoons

Olive oil, 2 tablespoons

Yellow onions, 2 large,
chopped (about 4 cups/
16 oz/500 g)

Apples (see note), 4 lb (2 kg),
peeled, cored, and chopped

Fresh mint, 3 tablespoons
chopped

Fresh thyme leaves,
1 tablespoon

MAKES 4 ONE-PINT
(16-FL OZ/500-ML) JARS

RHUBARB-MINT CHUTNEY

RHUBARB AFICIONADOS PRIZE THE SPRING VEGETABLE FOR ITS VIVID PINK HUE, ITS DISTINCTIVE TARTNESS, AND ITS JAMLIKE TEXTURE WHEN COOKED. HERE, A GENEROUS AMOUNT OF SUGAR AND MINT TEMPERS RHUBARB'S NATURAL ACIDITY. SERVE THE CHUTNEY WITH GRILLED LAMB CHOPS OR ROAST TURKEY.

Rhubarb, 1½ lb (750 g) (about 5 large stalks)

Whole cloves, 1½ teaspoons, lightly crushed

Olive oil, 1 tablespoon

Yellow onions, 2, coarsely chopped (about 3½ cups/ 14 oz/440 g)

Red plums, 4 (about 1 lb/ 14 oz/440 g), pitted and cut into large chunks

Orange zest, 1 tablespoon plus 1 teaspoon minced

White wine vinegar, ½ cup (4 fl oz/125 ml)

Sugar, ¼ cup (2 oz/60 g) plus 2 tablespoons

Salt, ¼ teaspoon

Freshly ground pepper, 1½ teaspoons

Fresh mint, ½ cup (¾ oz/20 g) coarsely chopped

MAKES 4 HALF-PINT (8-FL OZ/250-ML) JARS

Have ready 4 sterilized jars and their lids.

Trim the ends of the rhubarb stalks. Cut the stalks lengthwise into quarters, then cut crosswise into matchstick-size lengths.

Place the cloves on a square of cheesecloth, bring the corners together, and tie securely with kitchen string. In a large nonreactive saucepan over medium heat, warm the olive oil. Add the clove bundle, onions, plums, and orange zest and sauté until the onions are tender, about 10 minutes. Add the rhubarb, vinegar, sugar, salt, and pepper and cook, stirring occasionally, until the rhubarb is tender, about 10 minutes. Stir in the mint. Taste and adjust the seasoning.

Remove the clove bundle and ladle the hot chutney into the jars, leaving ¼ inch (6 mm) of headspace. Slide a metal chopstick or other thin tool down the side of each jar, between the glass and the chutney, four or five times. This will release any air bubbles. Adjust the headspace, if necessary, then wipe the rim of each jar clean and seal tightly with a lid.

Store the jars in the refrigerator for up to 1 month.

BACON-ONION JAM

THIS SWEET-SAVORY JAM, MADE WITH CARAMELIZED ONIONS, CIDER VINEGAR, AND BROWN SUGAR, IS MADE ALL THE BETTER WITH THE ADDITION OF APPLEWOOD-SMOKED BACON. IT'S DIVINE ON CRACKERS AND BISCUITS AND MAKES A LOVELY ADDITION TO CLUB SANDWICHES AND QUESADILLAS.

Preheat the oven to 400°F (200°C). Line a rimmed baking sheet with parchment paper. Place the bacon slices in a single layer on the baking sheet and bake, flipping the slices once with tongs after about 10 minutes, until browned and crisp, 15–20 minutes. Transfer the bacon to paper towels to drain, then crumble and set aside. Reserve 2 tablespoons of the drippings.

In a large sauté pan, heat the reserved drippings over medium-low heat. Add the onions and bay leaf, cover, and cook, stirring occasionally, until the onions are just beginning to brown, about 10 minutes. Uncover the pan, add 1 teaspoon of the brown sugar, the thyme, and the salt and cook uncovered, stirring frequently, until the onions are deep chestnut brown, about 15 minutes.

Reduce the heat to low and add the crumbled bacon, the remaining brown sugar, the vinegar, and the Worcestershire sauce. Cover and simmer, stirring frequently, until the flavors are blended and the jam has thickened, about 10 minutes. Remove from the heat, season with pepper, and taste and adjust the seasoning with salt. Remove the bay leaf.

Serve warm, or store in an airtight container in the refrigerator for up to 2 weeks, then bring to room temperature before serving.

Thick-sliced applewood smoked bacon, 1 pound (500 g)

Yellow onions, 2, finely chopped

Bay leaf, 1

Dark brown sugar, ¼ cup (2 oz/60 g) firmly packed plus 1 teaspoon

Fresh thyme leaves, 1 teaspoon

Salt, ¾ teaspoon

Cider vinegar, ¼ cup (2 fl oz/60 ml)

Worcestershire sauce, 2 teaspoons

Freshly ground pepper

MAKES 1½–1¾ CUPS (15–17 OZ/470–545 G)

SUN-DRIED TOMATO JAM

THIS EASY, SAVORY JAM IS A FANTASTIC WAY TO ENJOY THE DEEP AND ALMOST SMOKY FLAVOR OF TOMATOES THROUGHOUT THE YEAR. IT'S DELICIOUS SPREAD ON TOAST, AS AN ACCOMPANIMENT TO CHEESE, OR EVEN ATOP SCRAMBLED EGGS. IT ALSO MAKES A GREAT GIFT OVER THE HOLIDAYS.

Drained oil-packed sun-dried tomatoes, 2 cups (10 oz/315 g), coarsely chopped

Extra-virgin olive oil, 1 tablespoon

Garlic, 2 cloves, minced

Red onion, ½, thinly sliced

Sugar, 1 tablespoon

Red wine vinegar, ¼ cup (2 fl oz/60 ml)

Dried thyme, ½ teaspoon

Sea salt and freshly ground pepper

MAKES ABOUT 1 CUP (10 OZ/315 G)

In a saucepan over medium heat, combine the tomatoes, oil, garlic, and onion and cook, stirring, until the onion begins to brown, about 5 minutes. Stir in the sugar, vinegar, and thyme. Add 1 cup (8 fl oz/ 250 ml) water and ½ teaspoon each salt and pepper, bring to a boil, reduce the heat to low, cover, and simmer for 30 minutes. Uncover, raise the heat to medium-high, and cook until thick, about 5 minutes.

Let cool completely before serving. Tomato jam can be stored in the refrigerator in an airtight container for up to 2 weeks.

DRINKS
& MIXERS

LIMONCELLO

THIS SWEET, AROMATIC LIQUEUR IS SERVED AS AN AFTER-DINNER DRINK IN DAINTY CHILLED GLASSES ALL OVER ITALY. THE FLAVORS MELLOW OVER TIME, SO ALLOW THE LIQUEUR TO REST FOR A FEW WEEKS FOR THE BEST FLAVOR. TANGERINES OR BLOOD ORANGES CAN BE SUBSTITUTED.

Using a fine-tooth grater, zest the lemons over a large measuring cup with a spout. Add the vodka to the cup, then pour the mixture into a 1-qt (1-l) glass jar. Screw on the lid and place the jar in a cool, dark place for 30 days, shaking it every few days.

Strain the vodka mixture through a fine-mesh tea strainer or use the plunger of a spotlessly clean French press coffee maker. Alternatively, dampen a double layer of cheesecloth with cold water and wring out all of the moisture. Line a fine-mesh sieve with the cheesecloth and place over a large measuring cup. Pour the vodka mixture into the sieve and let it drain completely, pressing gently on the lemon zest.

Using a funnel, pour the strained liquor into a 4½-cup (36–fl oz/1.2-l) bottle. In a small saucepan, combine 1½ cups (12 fl oz/375 ml) water with the sugar and bring to a boil over medium-high heat, stirring until the sugar has dissolved. Remove the sugar syrup from the heat, add it to the vodka, secure the lid, and shake to blend. Refrigerate for at least 4 days; the liqueur will mellow in flavor with age. It will keep indefinitely in the refrigerator or freezer.

FOR GRAPPA SUNDROP: Mix together 3 fl oz (90 ml) Limoncello and ¾ fl oz (20 ml) grappa. Pour over crushed ice in a chilled martini glass and garnish with a lemon wedge. Makes 1 serving.

FOR SPARKLING LIMONCELLO: Add a splash of Limoncello to a chilled Champagne flute or coupe. Fill the glass with Champagne. Makes 1 serving.

Organic lemons, 2½ lb (1.25 kg)

Vodka, 1 bottle (24-fl oz/750-ml oz) 100-proof

Sugar, 1 cup (8 oz/250 g)

MAKES ABOUT 4½ CUPS (36 FL OZ/1.2 L)

CRANBERRY-POMEGRANATE SYRUP

IF YOU'RE A FAN OF SEA BREEZES, COSMOPOLITANS, OR CAPE COD COCKTAILS, YOU'LL WANT TO HAVE A BOTTLE OF THIS NOT-TOO-SWEET COCKTAIL MIXER ON HAND AT ALL TIMES. THANKS TO ITS RUBY RED COLOR AND FESTIVE FLAVOR, IT MAKES A NIFTY HOSTESS GIFT, SO YOU MAY WANT TO DOUBLE THE RECIPE.

**100% pomegranate juice,
1 cup (8 fl oz/250 ml)**

Star anise pod, 1

**100% cranberry juice,
2 cups (16 fl oz/500 ml)**

**Fresh tangerine juice, 1 cup
(8 fl oz/250 ml), strained**

**Agave syrup, ⅔ cup
(5 fl oz/150 g)**

MAKES 4 CUPS (32 FL OZ/1 L)

In a small saucepan, combine the pomegranate juice and star anise over medium heat and bring to a simmer. Remove from the heat and let stand for 1 hour.

Discard the star anise. In a pitcher, combine the pomegranate juice, cranberry juice, tangerine juice, and agave syrup and stir well. Pour the mixture into a clean 1-qt (1-l) jar and refrigerate for up to 2 months. Shake well before using.

FOR THE PERFECT COSMOPOLITAN COCKTAIL: Fill a cocktail shaker half full with ice. Add 2 parts Cranberry-Pomegranate Syrup and 1 part vodka, cover, and shake well. Strain into a chilled martini glass and serve.

MARGARITA MIX

MOST NEON YELLOW MARGARITA MIXES ARE MADE WITH HIGH-FRUCTOSE CORN SYRUP AND A LITANY OF CHEMICALS AND ARTIFICIAL FLAVORS. PERHAPS THAT'S WHY THEY TASTE A BIT LIKE CLEANING FLUID. THIS RECIPE CONTAINS NOTHING BUT FRESH CITRUS JUICES AND AGAVE SYRUP.

In a large nonreactive bowl, whisk together all of the ingredients until blended. Strain the mixture through a fine-mesh sieve into a pitcher, then pour into a bottle, cap tightly, and refrigerate until ready to serve. The mixer keeps for 2 weeks stored in the refrigerator.

FOR CADILLAC MARGARITAS: Fill a cocktail shaker half full with ice. Add 2 fl oz (60 ml) Margarita Mix, 2 fl oz (60 ml) tequila, and ½ fl oz (15 ml) Cointreau or triple sec, cover, and shake well. Pour into a tumbler over ice. Alternatively, in a blender, combine all of the ingredients with ½ cup (4 fl oz/125 ml) crushed ice and process until smooth, then pour into a tumbler. (For a salted rim, first moisten the rim of the tumbler with a lime wedge, then coat the rim with sea salt.)

Agave syrup, 1 cup
(8 fl oz/250 ml)

Filtered water, 1 cup
(8 fl oz/250 ml)

Fresh lemon juice, ½ cup
(4 fl oz/125 ml)

Fresh lime juice, ¼ cup
(2 fl oz/60 ml)

Fresh tangerine juice, ¼ cup
(2 fl oz/60 ml)

MAKES ABOUT 2¾ CUPS
(22 FL OZ/680 ML), ENOUGH
FOR 11 MARGARITAS

HORCHATA

A CREAMY NONDAIRY BEVERAGE MADE WITH RICE AND/OR ALMONDS OR OTHER NUTS OR SEEDS, HORCHATA IS POPULAR THROUGHOUT LATIN AMERICA. ITS CREAMY, SLIGHTLY SWEET FLAVOR IS PERFECT FOR TACO NIGHT, ESPECIALLY IF YOU'VE ADDED TOO MUCH HOT SAUCE.

Slivered blanched almonds, 2 cups (9 oz/280 g)

Sweet rice flour (preferably Mochiko brand), ¾ cup (4 oz/125 g)

Cinnamon sticks, 2, broken into pieces

Very hot water, 6 cups (48 fl oz/1.5 l)

Sugar, ⅔ cup (5 oz/155 g)

Ground cinnamon, for garnish

MAKES ABOUT 8 CUPS (64 FL OZ/2 L)

Preheat the oven to 350°F (180°C). Spread the almonds on a rimmed baking sheet and bake, stirring once, until lightly toasted, 15–20 minutes.

Transfer the almonds to a large bowl and add the rice flour, cinnamon sticks, and very hot water. Cover loosely and set aside at room temperature for at least 8 hours or for up to 16 hours.

Working in batches, transfer the rice-almond mixture (including the cinnamon pieces) to a blender and process until smooth. Dampen a thin dish towel or double layer of cheesecloth with cold water and wring out all of the moisture. Line a fine-mesh sieve with the towel or cheesecloth and set the sieve over a large pitcher or bowl. Pour the rice-almond mixture through the sieve and discard the solids.

In a small saucepan, combine the sugar with 1 cup (8 fl oz/250 ml) water and bring to a boil over medium-high heat, stirring to dissolve the sugar. Remove from the heat, add 3 cups (24 fl oz/750 ml) cold water to the pan, and stir well. Let cool. Add the sugar water to the strained rice-almond mixture and stir to blend.

To serve, pour over ice in tall glasses and garnish each serving with a pinch of cinnamon. Store in a covered container in the refrigerator for up to 1 week.

ALMOND NOG

NUTTY TASTING AND NOT TOO SWEET, THIS HOMEMADE DAIRY-FREE TWIST ON EGGNOG IS GREAT SERVED ALL BY ITSELF OVER ICE. DURING THE HOLIDAY SEASON, HOWEVER, A SHOT OF SPICED RUM IN EACH GLASS IS A FESTIVE AND WELCOME ADDITION.

Slivered blanched almonds, 2 cups (9 oz/280 g)

Medjool dates, 6, pitted

Boiling water, 6 cups (48 fl oz/1.5 l)

Agave syrup, ¼ cup (2 fl oz/60 ml)

Rum extract, ½ teaspoon

Nutmeg, ¼ to ½ teaspoon freshly grated

Cinnamon, ¼ teaspoon

MAKES ABOUT 6 CUPS (48 FL OZ/1.5 L)

Place the almonds and dates in a large heatproof bowl. Add the boiling water and let the mixture steep for 1 hour.

Working in batches, transfer the almonds, dates, and soaking water to a blender and process until smooth. Dampen a thin dish towel or double layer of cheesecloth with cold water and wring out all of the moisture. Line a fine-mesh sieve with the towel or cheesecloth and set the sieve over a large pitcher or bowl. Pour the almond-date mixture though the sieve. Gather up the ends of the towel, twist the ends together, and press out all of the liquid. Be patient and keep squeezing until all of the liquid has been extracted. You should have about 6 cups (48 fl oz/1.5 l) almond milk. Discard the solids, or dehydrate them and use them in a recipe that calls for almond flour.

Add the agave syrup, rum extract, nutmeg, and cinnamon to the almond milk and mix well. Serve in tumblers over ice, or store in a tightly covered container in the refrigerator for up to 2 weeks, then whisk well before serving.

SIMPLE SYRUP X 4

THIS BASIC RECIPE FOR PLAIN SUGAR SYRUP PROVIDES THE BASE FOR
ENDLESS VARIATIONS IN FLAVOR. USE THESE LUSCIOUS SIMPLE SYRUPS
TO BRIGHTEN SEASONAL COCKTAILS OR TRANSFORM NONALCOHOLIC DRINKS
INTO SOMETHING SPECIAL BY ADDING THEM TO SPARKLING WATER OR TEA.

In a small saucepan, combine the sugar and water over medium
heat and bring to a boil, stirring to dissolve the sugar. Remove from
the heat and let cool. Store in an airtight container in the refrigerator
for up to 3 weeks.

FOR ROSE SYRUP: Add 2 teaspoons rose water after removing
the simple syrup from the heat.

FOR ORANGE SYRUP: Add 2 teaspoons orange flower water after
removing the simple syrup from the heat.

FOR ELDER FLOWER SYRUP: Add 1 tablespoon loose dried elder
flowers or 1 tea bag elder flower tea after removing the simple
syrup from the heat. Let cool, then cover and refrigerate overnight.
The next day, strain the liquid through a fine-mesh sieve into
an airtight container and store in the refrigerator for up to 3 weeks.

FOR LIME SYRUP: Add 4 kaffir lime leaves and 1 strip lime zest,
about 2 inches (5 cm) long, or 1 lemongrass stalk, coarsely chopped,
after removing the simple syrup from the heat. Let cool, then cover
and refrigerate overnight. The next day, strain the liquid through a
fine-mesh sieve into an airtight container and store in the refrigerator
for up to 3 weeks.

Sugar, 1 cup (8 oz/250 g)

Water, 1 cup (8 fl oz/250 ml)

**MAKES ABOUT 1½ CUPS
(12 FL OZ/375 ML)**

HOMEMADE TONIC

TONIC WAS ORIGINALLY A HEALTH DRINK BECAUSE IT CONTAINED QUININE, A NATURAL MALARIA PREVENTATIVE. A SMART FELLOW DISCOVERED THAT TONIC TASTED MUCH BETTER MIXED WITH BOOZE, AND THE GIN AND TONIC WAS BORN. LOOK FOR CINCHONA POWDER AND CITRIC ACID AT HERB STORES OR ONLINE.

In a food processor, combine the sugar, lemongrass, and lime leaves and pulse until finely ground. Add the cinchona bark powder and citric acid powder and pulse to combine.

Using a fine-tooth grater, grate the zest from the lime and reserve. Halve and juice the lime and measure 2 tablespoons. In a large nonreactive saucepan, combine the sugar mixture, filtered water, lime juice, and zest. Bring to a simmer over medium heat, reduce the heat to maintain a low simmer, and cook uncovered, stirring occasionally, for 30 minutes.

Dampen a piece of cheesecloth with water, wring out all of the moisture, and line a fine-mesh sieve with it. Set the sieve over a pitcher or bowl and strain the mixture through the sieve, pressing on the solids to extract as much liquid as possible. Alternatively, strain the mixture through an extra-fine-mesh tea strainer. Transfer the syrup to a clean jar and refrigerate uncovered until cool. Screw on the cap, then store in the refrigerator for up to 2 months.

To make 1 cup (8 fl oz/250 ml) tonic, add 2–3 teaspoons of the syrup to 1 cup (8 fl oz/250 ml) soda water.

Sugar, 1 cup (8 oz/250 g)

Lemongrass, 3 stalks, root end and top two-thirds of stalk removed and bulb portion thinly sliced

Kaffir lime leaves, 12

Cinchona bark powder, 1 tablespoon

Citric acid powder, 2 tablespoons

Lime, 1

Filtered water, 1 cup (8 fl oz/250 ml)

MAKES ¾ CUP (6 FL OZ/185 ML) SYRUP

DRY MIXES & VARIATIONS

GINGERBREAD-SPICED APPLE PANCAKES

All-purpose flour, 2¼ cups (11½ oz/360 g)

Light brown sugar, ¼ cup (2 oz/60 g) firmly packed

Baking powder, 2 teaspoons

Baking soda, ¼ teaspoon

Ground cinnamon, ¼ teaspoon

Ground allspice, ½ teaspoon

Ground ginger, ½ teaspoon

Freshly grated nutmeg, ¼ teaspoon

Salt, ½ teaspoon

Stir together all ingredients and store in an airtight container.

To make the pancakes, combine the dry mix with 2 peeled and shredded apples, 1¾ cups (14 fl oz/430 ml) whole milk, 2 large eggs, and 2 tablespoons melted butter. Heat a lightly oiled griddle over high heat.

For each pancake, pour about ⅓ cup (3 fl oz/ 80 ml) of the batter onto the griddle. Cook until bubbles form and break on the surface, about 1½ minutes. Turn the pancakes and cook until golden brown on the second side, about 1 minute. Transfer to a platter. Repeat until all the batter is used, oiling the griddle as needed. Serve the pancakes with maple syrup.

MAKES ENOUGH MIX FOR ABOUT 4 SERVINGS

BUTTERMILK CORN BREAD

Yellow cornmeal, 2 cups (10 oz/315 g)

All-purpose flour, 1 cup (5 oz/155 g)

Sugar, ⅓ cup (3 oz/90 g)

Baking powder, 1 tablespoon

Salt, ¾ teaspoon

Baking soda, ½ teaspoon

Freshly ground pepper, 1 teaspoon

Stir together all ingredients and store in an airtight container.

To make the corn bread, preheat the oven to 400°F (200°C). Butter an 11-by-7-inch (28-by- 18-cm) baking dish. Using your fingertips, rub ½ cup (4 oz/125 g) cold unsalted butter, cut into small pieces, into the dry mix. Whisk together 1½ cups (12 fl oz/375 ml) buttermilk and 3 large eggs. Using a wooden spoon, stir the buttermilk mixture into the dry ingredients until thoroughly combined.

Transfer the batter to the prepared dish. Bake until the corn bread is golden brown on top and a toothpick inserted into the center comes out clean, about 30 minutes. Let cool in the pan on a wire rack. Cut the bread into squares and serve warm or at room temperature.

FOR HERBED CORN BREAD: Add 1 teaspoon each dried sage and marjoram.

MAKES ENOUGH MIX FOR ABOUT 8-10 SERVINGS

IRISH SODA BREAD

Unbleached bread flour, 2¼ cups (11½ oz/360 g)

Old-fashioned rolled oats, ½ cup (1½ oz/45 g)

Wheat bran, ¼ cup (½ oz/15 g)

Baking soda, 1½ teaspoons

Salt, 1 teaspoon

Stir together all ingredients and store in an airtight container.

To make the bread, place a large baking sheet in the oven and preheat the oven to 425°F (220°C). Using your fingertips, rub 4 tablespoons (2 oz/ 60 g) cold unsalted butter, cut into small pieces, into the dry mix until the mixture resembles coarse meal. Add 1½ cups (12 oz/375 g) plain low-fat yogurt and quickly stir to blend the ingredients as evenly as possible, forming a rough ball.

Lightly dust a clean work surface with flour and set the ball of dough on it. Flatten the ball slightly into a 7-inch (18-cm) dome and sprinkle it with flour, spreading it lightly over the surface with your fingertips. Using a sharp knife, cut a shallow X from one side of the loaf to the other.

Remove the baking sheet from the oven. Using a large metal spatula, transfer the loaf to the preheated baking sheet. Bake until well risen, brown, and crusty, 30–35 minutes. Transfer the loaf to a wire rack to cool slightly before serving.

MAKES ENOUGH MIX FOR 1 ROUND LOAF

OATMEAL COOKIES

Old-fashioned rolled oats, 1 cup (3 oz/90 g)

Sugar, 1 cup (8 oz/250 g)

All-purpose flour, 2 tablespoons plus 2 teaspoons

Salt, ½ teaspoon

Baking powder, ½ teaspoon

Vanilla bean, 1

Stir together all ingredients and store in an airtight container.

To make the cookies, preheat the oven to 325°F (165°C). Line 2 baking sheets with parchment paper. Remove the vanilla bean and combine the mix with 1 beaten large egg and ½ cup (4 oz/ 125 g) melted and cooled butter. Let the batter rest, stirring occasionally, until thickened, 15–20 minutes.

Drop the batter by the teaspoon onto the baking sheets, spacing the mounds 2½ inches (6 cm) apart. Bake until the cookies are golden, 8–12 minutes. Let cool on a rack until firm, about 5 minutes, before serving.

MAKES ENOUGH MIX FOR ABOUT 12 COOKIES

RAISIN SPICE MUFFINS

All-purpose flour, 2 cups (10 oz/315 g)

Sugar, ⅔ cup (5 oz/155 g)

Baking powder, 1 tablespoon

Salt, 1 teaspoon

Freshly ground nutmeg, 1 teaspoon

Ground cinnamon, 1 teaspoon

Ground cloves, ½ teaspoon

Ground allspice, ½ teaspoon

Dark or golden raisins, ¼ cup (1½ oz/45 g)

Stir together all ingredients and store in an airtight container.

To make the muffins, preheat the oven to 400°F (200°C). Butter 12 standard muffin cups. Whisk together 1 large egg, 1 cup (8 fl oz/250 ml) heavy cream, ½ cup (4 fl oz/125 ml) whole milk, and ⅓ cup (3 oz/90 g) melted unsalted butter. Mix and combine with the flour mixture. Spoon the batter into the muffin cups, filling them two-thirds full. Bake until a toothpick inserted into the center of a muffin comes out clean, about 20 minutes. Let cool in the pan for 3–5 minutes, then turn out and serve.

MAKES ENOUGH MIX FOR 12 MUFFINS

BREADCRUMBS

Coarse country bread, 3 thick slices

Garlic, 3 cloves

Sea salt and freshly ground pepper

Extra-virgin olive oil, 2 tablespoons

Discard the crusts and tear the bread into chunks. In a food processor, pulse the garlic until minced. Add the bread, ½ teaspoon salt, and a pinch of pepper. Pulse until coarse crumbs form. In a small nonstick frying pan, warm the oil over medium heat. Add the crumb mixture and cook, stirring, until crisp and golden brown, 2–3 minutes. Store in an airtight container in the freezer for up to 6 months.

MAKES ABOUT 1 CUP (4 OZ/125 G)

REAL CHAI TEA MIX

Fennel seeds, 1 teaspoon

Green cardamom pods, 3, split

Peppercorns, coriander seeds, whole cloves, 8 each

Cinnamon stick, 1

Ground ginger, 1 teaspoon

Loose-leaf Assam tea, 2 tablespoons

Preheat the oven to 350°F (180°C). Combine the fennel, cardamom, peppercorns, coriander, cloves, and cinnamon in a pie pan and toast until fragrant, about 5 minutes. Pour into a bowl to cool, then crush lightly with the back of a wooden spoon. Stir in the ginger and tea. Store the mix in an airtight container. To make chai tea, in a small saucepan, combine the dry mix with 2 cups (16 fl oz/500 ml) each whole milk and water and bring just to a boil over medium-high heat. Immediately remove from the heat, cover, and let steep for about 20 minutes. Strain through a fine-mesh sieve into cups and sweeten with sugar or honey to taste. Serve right away.

FOR VANILLA CHAI: Add a 1-inch (2.5-cm) piece vanilla bean to the dry mix with the tea.

FOR SPICED COCOA: Add 3 oz (90 g) chopped bittersweet chocolate, in place of the tea.

MAKES ENOUGH MIX FOR 4-6 SERVINGS

BARBECUE SEASONING

Sea salt, 3 tablespoons

Ground white pepper, 1 tablespoon

Paprika, 1 tablespoon

Granulated garlic, 1 tablespoon

Dried thyme, 1 tablespoon

Red pepper flakes, 1 teaspoon

Stir together all ingredients and store in an airtight container for up to 1 year.

MAKES ABOUT ½ CUP (1½ OZ/45 G)

MARSHMALLOW VARIATIONS

Prepare the Vanilla Marshmallows as directed on page 90. When the mixture becomes white and thick, mix in one of the following flavors or a color.

COCOA MARSHMALLOWS: Omit the vanilla and whip in 2 tablespoons unsweetened cocoa powder.

MINT MARSHMALLOWS: Omit the vanilla and whip in ½ teaspoon pure peppermint extract.

RAINBOW MARSHMALLOWS: Use high-quality liquid or gel food coloring and select any color you like. Add the coloring, a few drops at a time, until you achieve the color intensity desired.

SEEDED CRACKER VARIATIONS

Prepare the Seeded Crackers as directed on page 56, making one of the following changes:

LEMON THYME CRACKERS: Omit the poppy, sesame, and mustard seeds. Add the grated zest of 1 lemon and 1 tablespoon chopped fresh thyme with the pepper.

OREGANO-PARMESAN CRACKERS: Omit the poppy, sesame, and mustard seeds. Add 1 tablespoon chopped fresh oregano and 2 tablespoons grated Parmesan cheese with the pepper.

JACK CHEESE CRACKERS: Omit the pepper, poppy, and sesame seeds. Add 2 tablespoons grated dry Jack cheese with the mustard seeds.

SPICY CHEESE CRACKERS: Omit the coarsely gound pepper, poppy, and sesame seeds. Add 1 teaspoon ground cayenne pepper, 1 teaspoon paprika, and 2 tablespoons grated dry jack cheese with the mustard seeds.

INDEX

weldonowen

415 Jackson Street, Suite 200, San Francisco, CA 94111

www.weldonowen.com

BETTER FROM SCRATCH

Conceived and produced by Weldon Owen, Inc.
In collaboration with Williams-Sonoma, Inc.
3250 Van Ness Avenue, San Francisco, CA 94109

A WELDON OWEN PRODUCTION

Printed and bound in China by 1010 Printing, Ltd.

First printed in 2014

10 9 8 7 6 5 4 3 2 1

Library of Congress Control Number: 2014931494

ISBN 13: 978-1-61628-731-3
ISBN 10: 1-61628-731-4

Weldon Owen is a division of
BONNIER

WELDON OWEN, INC

CEO and President Terry Newell
VP, Sales and Marketing Amy Kaneko
VP, Publisher Roger Shaw

Associate Publisher Amy Marr
Assistant Editor Emma Rudolph

Creative Director Kelly Booth
Art Director Ashley Lima
Designer Rachel Lopez Metzger

Production Director Chris Hemesath
Associate Production Director Michelle Duggan

Photographer Alice Gao
Food Stylist Lilian Kang
Prop Stylist Christine Wolheim

Additional photography by: Petrina Tinslay:
page 33; Ray Katchatorian: pages 48 and 112.

Front cover photograph by: Ashley Lima

ACKNOWLEDGEMENTS
Weldon Owen wishes to thank the following people for their
generous support in producing this book: Rachel Boller, Casey Catelli,
Marisa Kwek, Eve Lynch, Elizabeth Parsons, and Sharon Silva